CALLED FOR TRAVELLING

OTHER BOOKS BY RON RAPOPORT:

High for the Game (with Chip Oliver)

Love in the NBA (with Stan Love)

CALLED FOR

TRAVELLING

Jim McGregor and Ron Rapoport

MACMILLAN PUBLISHING CO., INC.

New York

FOR MY MOTHER,
who has given fifty-five years
of love and affection.
AND FOR RENA,
who has given ten years
of wonder and joy.
—JIM MCGREGOR

Copyright © 1978 by Jim McGregor and Ron Rapoport

All rights reserved. No part of this book may be reproduced or transmitted in any form or by any means, electronic or mechanical, including photocopying, recording or by any information storage and retrieval system, without permission in writing from the Publisher.

Macmillan Publishing Co., Inc.
866 Third Avenue, New York, N.Y. 10022
Collier Macmillan Canada, Ltd.

Library of Congress Cataloging in Publication Data

McGregor, Jim.
    Called for travelling.

    1. McGregor, Jim. 2. Basketball coaches—United States—Biography. I. Rapoport, Ron, joint author.
II. Title.
GV884.M25A33   796.32'3'0924 [B]   78–9430
ISBN 0–02–583350–2

First Printing 1978

Printed in the United States of America

Contents

Acknowledgments

It is customary to say that the people who have contributed to a book like this are too numerous to mention. That is literally true in this case, but I am going to try, anyhow.

To the players who took the time to answer their old coach's request for rosters, data and remembered experiences . . .

To the 600 who participated on the various tours over the years . . .

To the 250 on the various national teams I coached . . .

To the sponsors, God bless them . . .

To Les Powell, whose death in Vietnam in 1968—a year after he toured with us—brought the Southeast Asian jungles to Europe in the most vivid way . . .

To Italy, which produced the Italians . . .

To Aldo Giordani, Pierre Tessier and Marco Cassini, who make basketball live for the readers of Europe . . .

To R. W. Jones, a genius to whom every basketball man is in debt . . .

Grazia, merci et danke.

Introduction

JIM MCGREGOR IS fifty-five years old, five feet eight, mostly bald and, despite a daily one-mile swim, losing his battle against middle-aged paunch. In other words, he is never likely to be mistaken for Julius Erving.

Yet, should he and Dr. J. ever find themselves walking together down the streets of Hälsingborg, Sweden; Pesaro, Italy; or Iquitos, Peru—not to mention Stockholm, Rome or Lima—the response of passersby might very likely be, "Who's that big guy with Jim McGregor?"

Twenty-five years of travelling the world as a basketball coach may not have done much to make McGregor a household word in the country of his birth, but there is hardly a one outside the United States where this native of Portland, Oregon, has not left his mark. He is, quite simply, the best-known basketball personality in the world.

He has taught the Poles and the Russians, the Italians and the Greeks, the Swedes and the Peruvians and the Filipinos. He has given clinics for the Watusis in Africa and for the Indians at the headwaters of the Amazon. He has coached the national teams of eight countries and been decorated by five of them. In recent years, foreign nations have come to him each summer at his international basketball camp in Long Beach, California.

However, for the past decade, McGregor has done more than coach foreign teams and hold clinics in out-of-the-way places. He has become the Pied Piper of Basketball, leading an ever-changing team of American players on a never-ending tour of the globe. Sponsored by United States and multinational corporations, and playing local teams in cities large and small, McGregor's teams comprise the world's tallest tour group.

Not that his players remain tourists for long. Most of them find jobs in foreign countries and, as a result, there are American players on local teams all over the world. For each player who is left behind as the tour pushes on, another comes over from the United States to take his place. France's authoritative sports newspaper, *L'Equipe*, once dubbed McGregor "The Merchant of Happiness." McGregor's teams have played some 2,000 games in the last ten years and the tour has taken them from above the Arctic Circle to the southernmost reaches of Chile, from Madrid to Manila and back again.

"I think it is fair to say that my teams have played basketball in every conceivable place where it could be played," McGregor says, "and in some that were inconceivable. We've played in the original Olympic stadium in Greece, in the courtyard of a palace in Istanbul and in a church in Venice that was converted into a basketball arena. We've played on an oil tanker in a bay off the Irish coast and on the stage of the Albert Hall in London where the spectators sat high up in the boxes and each player had a private dressing room complete with mirror and makeup lights.

"In Italy, we've played in the Roman arena in Verona where they have famous music festivals and opera performances, in an abandoned cavalry training hall in Rome and in the courtyard of the municipal building in Bologna. We've played on an ice rink in Helsinki where it was so cold the players on the bench had to stamp their feet for warmth. And we've played on a roller-skating rink in Portugal where there was still salt on the floor to keep the wheels from slipping.

"We've played in places where we outnumbered the crowd and we've played before a hundred and fifty thousand people in St. Peter's Square. Of course, some of them may have come to see the Pope."

It seems only right that, with this book, Jim McGregor should at long last bring his act back home.

RON RAPOPORT
EVANSTON, ILLINOIS

PART ONE

Follow the Bouncing Ball

CHAPTER I

Leaving Spokane

When I walked into the president's office, I knew exactly what I was going to say.

Listen, I was going to say, when you brought me here, Whitworth College was a small fundamentalist Christian college in eastern Washington with a beautiful campus and a terrible basketball team. Now, three years later, the religious emphasis is the same, the campus is still beautiful and the basketball team is terrific. I've recruited some fine players. We've won seventy-six games in three years and the conference title twice. We've made it to the quarterfinals of the national small-college tournament. We've won games against major universities like Washington State and Montana that we'd never beaten before. And yesterday I was named Coach of the Year.

Now I'd like to talk to you about my budget for next year. First, I want twenty scholarships. This will cost us $50,000, which is five times what we spent when I came here. But our basketball receipts are way up and the booster club I organized in Spokane is coming through with a lot of donations. And second, there is the matter of my three-year contract being up, so perhaps we ought to talk about signing a new one.

That is what I was going to say. I never got the chance. The president did all the talking.

"Jim," he said, "we're not going to renew your contract. The board of trustees wants to thank you very much. You've fulfilled all the terms of your contract, but we're going to take this program in a different direction."

And that was that. Coach of the Year one day. Out of a job the next. I should not have been surprised. All the signs had been there for a long time. But when you are thirty-two years old and full of yourself, you don't worry about warning signals. You figure that being a winner solves all problems. Well, believe me Vince Lombardi, winning is not the only thing.

I had gone to Whitworth in 1950 with a new wife and a new Plymouth, financed on ninety-nine easy monthly payments. The Plymouth, that is, not the wife. At the age of twenty-nine, I was possibly the youngest head basketball coach and athletic director in the country. Whitworth's president, Frank Warren, had wanted to boost the prestige of the college by changing its doormat athletic image. Though he was a born-again type of fundamentalist, he felt there was no reason a good Christian could not be a good athlete and vice versa.

Warren had been impressed by the University of Southern California's athletic tradition so he had written to Sam Barry, the basketball coach there, asking if there were any bright young coaches around. I had never been good enough to play basketball for Sam, but I had hung around and scouted for him. After I had gotten out of school, he had helped to get me the job as freshman track coach. The fact that the team was undefeated has always looked good on my résumé and I have never made a big point of saying that it had been that way for a decade before I got there and remained so for a decade after I left. At any rate, Sam's recommendation was good enough for Warren. I asked for a free hand in fund-raising and recruiting, got it and went to work.

Whitworth's initial need was players and I was determined to use every edge that I could find. It did not take me long to find one. One of my first speeches was given to the Spokane Kiwanis

Club, which I hoped to enlist in my efforts to create a booster club. The president of the organization, for his part, wanted me to know of its good works. There was one program he was particularly proud of—Homes for Widowed Mothers. I could hardly believe my ears.

"You mean, if I found a great basketball player whose mother was a widow," I said, "you would find her a home?"

"Sure," he said.

"Hold one," I said.

And I went out and found Phil Jordan. He had everything I could have asked: seven feet in height, enough talent to take him to the NBA eventually and a widowed mother. No sooner was it announced that Phil was coming to Whitworth, however, than I had my first encounter with controversy. I had enrolled him, it was said, by getting his mother a house, which was unfair recruiting. Nonsense, I said. It was merely a utilization of community assets.

That was just the beginning. Ralph Polson was a big junior-college center from Riverside, California, and a lot of schools were after him. I discovered another member of the team, however, who was only a fair player but was Ralph's best friend. I proposed a package deal and they both came. This time the screams were really loud: "How come a quality player like Ralph isn't going to UCLA or USC or Stanford? Where the hell is Whitworth? What's going on up there?"

At USC I found a fine football player who was flunking out. Even though grade requirements were not as strict at Whitworth, his transcript was so bad that I carried it up by hand to enter a personal plea, rather than entrust it to the mails. But he got into Whitworth and turned out to be a fine basketball player, too.

On top of everything else, I got lucky. Jim Doherty had started out at the University of Minnesota, but was attracted by Whitworth's religious emphasis. So he just showed up on my doorstep. Throw in a pair of twins from Idaho, Ray and Roy Beech, who brought teamwork and desire along with them, and Whitworth suddenly had a hell of a basketball team.

I was not averse to letting anyone know it, either. I would

stand up at press luncheons and say, "Well, tonight we play Eastern Washington and, gee, I hope they show up."

I was just as boyishly charming on the court, too. I am quite sure I established the American record for most technical fouls in one game during my tenure. We were playing the University of Puget Sound, which had a very good six-foot, ten-inch center named Gibbs. He was a little awkward on defense, though, and I thought that if we pressured him we might be able to get him to foul out. Sure enough, the score was close and there was still plenty of time left when Gibbs got his fourth foul.

My floor leader at the time was Ed Kretz, a short, stumpy guy, and he was racing down the court on a fast break when he heard the loud clomp of Gibbs close behind him. Kretz alertly decided this was his chance so he suddenly just stopped and crouched, figuring Gibbs would run into him and foul out.

Gibbs ran into him, all right. In fact, Gibbs knocked him down and rolled over on top of him. As they lay there together on the floor, there was not a single part of Kretz' body that was not being touched by some portion of Gibbs' anatomy. Only one element was missing from this little tableau—a whistle. The referee just stood there.

I rushed out onto the floor screaming, "Damn, that's either a foul or sodomy! You've got to call something!"

The referee pointed at me and said, "Oh, it's a foul, all right. A technical foul on you."

"That's the first thing you've called right tonight!" I shouted.

"And furthermore," he said, "it's going to be a technical foul for every second you're out here on this floor."

"I'm going to stay out here until I get my man out from under this mountain," I said, but all the time he was counting away, " '... two ... three ... four ...' " By the time he reached twelve, I had made it back to the bench, still shouting and pointing. Puget Sound's best free-throw shooter took twelve technical foul shots. Needless to say, we lost the game.

This sort of behavior did not go unnoticed by my coaching

colleagues, many of whom had been at their schools for years and had definite opinions of the way young coaches ought to act. The fact that they were used to Whitworth's being an easy win for them did not make them feel any more kindly toward me when we started knocking them off.

Some of the non-conference schools we had traditionally played suddenly found they did not have a place for us on their schedules any longer, and the colleges in the Evergreen Conference began to talk about changing recruiting regulations and entrance requirements. The other schools were also made nervous by the fact that I was raising a lot of money from the booster club I had organized. In the past, all donations had gone to the college's general fund and then been parcelled out to the athletic department by the administration. Now, however, the money went through me. There was never a hint of any impropriety and the books were always open to administration checks, but it was still another different way of doing things.

The biggest sin I committed, however, was in my relationship to the rest of the college. Whitworth was a devoutly religious school. The faculty believed deeply in its precepts and often made monetary sacrifices to teach there. There was no smoking, no drinking, no dancing. The emphasis was on modest living and devotion to God. But here was the new basketball coach joining the country club, wheeling and dealing with his booster club and running off around the country to hunt up basketball players regardless of whether or not they were the type of students who would normally attend a school like Whitworth.

My office was next door to the chapel and both students and faculty were required to hear the religious speakers who were brought in about once a week. I never did. Several times, Frank Warren mentioned this to me—that I was not leading what he liked to call "the exemplary Christian life," that I was not making my "testimony"—but it all went right over my head. I was doing what I had been brought there to do. The team was winning, the gym was full, Whitworth was being talked about all over the

Northwest. My friends thought Warren was trying to run the athletic department. His friends thought I was trying to run the university.

Once Warren realized that I was never going to project the image he wanted in his coach, we began to grow farther apart. My scheduling bothered him, for instance. Why were we playing Hawaii and Florida, he wanted to know, instead of Washington State and Montana? My answer—that trips were a prime recruiting inducement and that some of our traditional rivals did not want to play us after they discovered we were not an automatic win—did not convince him.

The moment I finally realized there was no way we could communicate came after he read a newspaper account of one of our games. The article pointed out that my strategy had been to lure the other team's star player into fouling out. This, Warren said, was unchristian conduct. No amount of protest on my part—defending it as sound basketball strategy and in no way unethical —could sway him.

The final scene came when Warren decided to seek outside guidance. Eventually, I am sure, he discussed the situation with God, but first he went to a more mundane source: one of my rival coaches, a man I had been beating. More in sorrow than in anger, the coach confirmed Warren's judgment that I was not the right type to be coaching at Whitworth.

So I was gone.

At first, I wasn't worried about getting another job. Nobody could take away my record at Whitworth and, in fact, I was soon hot on the trail of another good coaching position. In 1953, we had reached the quarterfinals of the National Association of Intercollegiate Athletics (NAIA) tournament in Kansas City and Southwest Missouri State, which had won the title, was about to lose its coach, Bob Vanatta, to West Point. I applied and soon heard through the grapevine that I was the number-one choice to replace Vanatta. The athletic director was bubbling about getting me and everybody along the line, including the president of the school, told me not to worry, approval was just a formality, the job was mine. But soon I stopped hearing from them and then the job went to somebody else. Later, I was put in touch with another school and again things looked very favorable. Once more, somebody else was hired.

It did not take a genius to figure out what had happened. They had called or written Whitworth to check up on me. If I was ever to coach again, I soon realized, I would have to go away somewhere—somewhere they did not know English.

CHAPTER **2**

On the Road

Dear ———— Airlines:

I would like to be appointed your international sports travel representative for the purpose of furthering travel by sports groups over your routes. I would accept such a position on the basis of a percentage of the business I am able to bring to you. . . .

I WROTE THAT LETTER fifty times and sent it to every international airline then in operation. I had no way of knowing how the idea would be received, but figured that my offer to work for only a percentage would demonstrate how confident I was that I could drum up enough business to make a living. The airlines, really, had nothing to lose. It was worth a chance.

Still, I was overjoyed when, in a very short time, I received a letter from Canadian Pacific Airlines offering me the job. I went up to the Vancouver office, discussed the details and accepted. I came home to find several more letters also offering jobs. In the next two or three weeks, I heard from virtually every airline I had written and they *all* offered me a job. I had panicked and taken the first one that had come along, but it was all right with me. I told my wife to stay with her mother for a while and I was off to see the world.

The World Basketball Championships, to be held in Rio de

Janeiro in 1954, were my first target. Were there any Asian countries—serviced by Canadian Pacific, of course—that might be interested in competing there? I got in touch with the basketball federations of several of them and found two likely prospects: Formosa and the Phillipines. There was only one problem. They could not afford it.

I'll tell you what, I wrote them. You travel Canadian Pacific to Vancouver and then barnstorm your way through the United States and Latin America to Brazil. I will schedule games with local teams for you en route that will earn enough money to pay your expenses. Done, said Formosa and the Phillipines. Canadian Pacific got a healthy bit of business and I was a basketball promoter. All I had to do now was set up the games to be played on the road to Rio.

At first, it was easy. There were plenty of college teams in the Pacific Northwest that were eager to play exhibition games against the two countries and the large Chinese community in New York made a game there look very profitable. Cuba was interested in playing the Formosans—this was before Castro—and so were Mexico and several other Latin American countries. In a very short time, I had set up fifteen to twenty games for both teams.

It was at that point that I had my first brush with the Amateur Athletic Union; in a later chapter, I will describe with all the venom at my command the length and scope of my battle with these people. For now, I will confine myself to this initial skirmish. It is not a bad introduction to the AAU mentality, as a matter of fact.

The moment the AAU heard about the games I had scheduled in the United States for the Philippines and Formosa, it refused to sanction them. The AAU, the authorized U.S. representative of the international basketball federation, often threatened to strip any American who defied it of his amateur standing.

I asked the AAU why it would not sanction the games. Because it had not originated them, it responded. I asked what difference that made. The Formosans wanted to play. The Filipinos wanted to play. The American teams wanted to play. People wanted to see them play. So why shouldn't they play? The AAU was un-moved. If it had not originated the games, the games would not take place. It was as simple as that. All the college teams I had scheduled backed out and the game in New York was cancelled. The Chinese promoters who were backing it there were furious, but the AAU could not have cared less.

I was left with only a few games on the West Coast against players who cared little about amateur standing since they were not exactly of Olympic caliber. In Portland, for a game against the Filipinos, we drew a grand total of thirty spectators and the promoter had to come up with the $500 guarantee out of his own pocket. I really felt sorry for him. I probably would have even if I had not been the promoter. We had a slightly better crowd in San Francisco, where there was a substantial Filipino population, but my first experience promoting basketball in the United States was a disaster.

After we left the States, however, things went much better. We had 5,000 people in Mexico City for the Filipinos and there was a great crowd in Havana for the Formosans. When I went to the box office afterwards to collect my share of the gate re-ceipts, I found myself staring into the face of the man who was in charge of sports in Cuba at the time.

"It's customary here that I get a percentage," he said, as I was handed my cut, "in recognition of my contribution to the game."

He had four things in his favor that I could see. One, he was a major in the Cuban army. Two, he had a very determined look on his face. Three, he was related to Batista. And four, he had a gun on his hip. He didn't mention the figure he had in mind, so I just took a wild stab at it and gave him fifteen percent, wondering if the tip one would give to an American waiter would satisfy him. It did and we got the hell out of Cuba.

Part of the reason for the success of our Latin American tour was the large Chinese community in many of the cities we played. Sometimes it was hard to tell how large. In Caracas, for instance, a man with an Oriental face approached us to play in another Venezuelan town, Valencia. Our game in Caracas had not drawn very well and when I checked I found there were only a few hundred Chinese living in Valencia. Also, it would cost quite a bit to transport the team there. But the man offered to take care of the expenses and even included a small guarantee. When we arrived in Valencia, we found a nice new arena jammed with 10,000 people. One look was enough to tell they were not native Venezuelans.

"What is this?" I asked the man. "There aren't supposed to be this many Chinese in the whole country."

He just smiled and said there weren't. Not legally. But as soon as one person came over, he would send his passport back home for somebody else to use. To the Venezuelan customs men, I guess, all Chinese looked alike.

The game was a big success, as was the Formosan team's tour throughout Latin America where Chinese immigrants came out in full force. Both teams played well when they got to Rio, too.

It was in this tournament that I got my first look at U.S. participation in major foreign competition. And my last look at a U.S. victory in the world championships. The tournament win in Rio was the end of American domination of the most important event in international basketball outside of the Olympics. Our failures since then are a tribute to the importance that is placed on the tournament by those in charge of amateur basketball in this country.

Garland Pinholster, a fine young coach from Oglethorpe University in Georgia, was handling the U.S. team, but he did not have much practice time and was frustrated at his inability to install his own system. When his team wound up losing games to the Soviet Union, Yugoslavia and Brazil, Pinholster got terribly depressed. Pete Newell, the famous University of California coach and a friend of mine, and I were so concerned about Pinholster that we walked him around the streets of Rio most of the night for fear he would do something drastic.

The tournament wound up with a great deal of significance for me. It was there that I first ran into the man who may have had as great an effect on my life as anyone I have ever known.

His name is R. William Jones and he is, quite simply, the single most powerful man in the history of basketball. James Naismith may have invented the game, but Jones, in his capacity as executive secretary of the International Basketball Federation, spread it around the world.

Jones is an Englishman who was born in Turkey and has lived all over the world. He speaks at least a dozen languages and has unlimited entrée to international sports circles. He was a brigadier general in the British Army during World War II, and some people believe he was a top official in British intelligence. As a young man, he attended Springfield College in Massachusetts, where Naismith hung up the first peach basket. Shortly after that Jones became general secretary for the YMCA, the organization that really introduced basketball around the world. Jones' contribution through the YMCA was twofold. He encouraged his people to teach the game abroad and he influenced many countries to organize national federations. When he started, there were perhaps fifteen countries that belonged to FIBA, the international basketball federation. Today, there are 143.

Jones also organized international European championships, Caribbean championships, Balkan championships and so on, until there were important regional tournaments being held regularly all over the world. In addition, he set up the world tournament that is now international basketball's biggest event and he lobbied for the sport's inclusion in the Olympics, an important element in increasing interest.

Jones was a master of timing. While the game was growing, he didn't put up any artificial barriers. Many cities, even some large ones, had no decent indoor arenas in the early days, and to draw crowds they often played outdoors—not always in the summer or in southern Europe. I have watched outdoor games in places like Belgium and northern Italy where it was cold, windy and wet. But as the game became more popular, Jones began insisting that important tournaments be played indoors and this encouraged the construction of modern arenas all over the European continent. He always knew when it was time to go after a new objective and when it was time to wait.

When I met Jones, I told him of my aim to coach internationally and asked if he knew of any jobs that might be available. He may have been impressed that I had helped Formosa and the Philippines to play in the tournament; at any rate he said that as a matter of fact there was a position open. Italy was looking for a coach for its national team. Why didn't I apply?

"What are the requirements?" I asked.

"A good coaching record and the ability to speak Italian," he said.

I figured one out of two wasn't bad.

CHAPTER 3

Parla Italiano?

I WASN'T ABOUT TO LET THE FACT that I didn't speak the language stop me. I assumed I was at least as smart as the average three-year-old Italian and I could learn it. The immediate task was to get the job.

The porter at my hotel in Rio did speak Italian and between the two of us we composed a telegram announcing my candidacy. It just so happened, I told the Italian federation, that I would be giving a clinic in Iran the following month and I would be glad to stop by to see them on my way back. This was a total fabrication, but I didn't want to seem overly anxious. And it worked. A date was set for an interview.

I went home to Portland and started a cram course in Italian. This wasn't easy since there was no place to learn it. The foreign-language boom hadn't begun yet, and I couldn't even find a teach-yourself-Italian book in the library. So I did the next best thing. I taught myself Spanish. I got records and books and worked with them day and night. The pronunciation of the two languages is different, of course, but much of the vocabulary is the same. I was counting on that, and on a book I had read about the Italian temperament, to pull me through.

The essence of getting along in Italy, this book said, is to be polite and never embarrass anybody. So when I got there, I made sure not to embarrass anybody. I said nothing at all if I could possibly help it. Luckily, the people I dealt with were more than happy to fill in the pauses. I found the Italians to be an exuberant, outgoing people who loved to sit and talk. Nothing seemed to please them more than having someone just listen. So I arrived with my fifty words of Italian and said almost nothing, except to repeat what was being said to me. Nine out of ten times this worked. If someone asked me a question, I would say, "Si," and then repeat what I had been asked, even though I didn't know what I was saying. It was only later that I would learn I had said, "Yes, I am hungry," or, "Yes, I would like to go back to the hotel, now."

But the Italian basketball officials didn't expect me to be fluent and they were impressed by my good coaching record at Whitworth, my recommendation from R. W. Jones and my international airlines connection, which I suppose they interpreted as the sign of a world traveller. After several meetings and many "Si's," I was hired as coach of the Italian national basketball team. Nearly twenty-five years later, I still regard that as the greatest single piece of good fortune I have ever had.

After a quick trip home, I arrived back in Italy ready to go to work. I went to the basketball federation headquarters and was told, "You've had a long hard trip. Get yourself organized, find an apartment and settle in. We'll call you when we need you."

The next time I heard from them was five months later. My only duties in the meantime were to watch the various Italian club teams play each Sunday so I could appraise some of the players who would be on the national team. I travelled all over the country, attending games and making notes on players. The other six days a week, I had nothing to do but learn Italian, pick up my paycheck and enjoy myself. I did all three religiously.

Now that I was living in Italy, I found it much easier to learn the language. In fact, the more time I spent out of the United States, the more rapidly I began to pick up additional languages.

Through the years, I would have a chance to study many of them intensely. In Peru, of all places, there was a French institute. In Turkey, I not only learned some Turkish, but I also found a German institute where I studied a language I had begun to pick up when I awakened to the influx of German girls into Italy. The seven months I spent in an Austrian hospital—where only one or two of the doctors spoke English—didn't hurt my German, either.

One advantage I have had in learning languages is that the key terms of my trade tend to be similar from one tongue to the next. The word for dribble, for instance, is *dribbler* in French, *driblar* in Spanish and *driblare* in Italian. The same holds true for many other basketball words. Sometimes, even the nuances of the terminology translate fairly closely. In Italian, the word for guard is *regista*, which can also mean conductor of an orchestra or director of a play. Very often, we will call a guard a playmaker so the thought is quite similar. Other times, international basketball simply defers to English usage. Thus, while calling a time out, the Italians say "*Minuto*," but they put their hands up in the form of a T, the way American coaches do when calling time.

But no matter how many languages I learned, or how widespread the use of English became in the world, there were still times when I ran into problems.

In 1956, the Formosan basketball federation invited me to coach a team that was preparing for the Asian Games. Chinese citizens from all over the Far East—except the mainland, of course—were invited since the team was supposed to represent all of China. There were players from Vietnam, Singapore, Thailand, the Philippines and Hong Kong, each with his own language. We had one player who spoke Mandarin, another who spoke Cantonese and one whose only language was French, as well as several who spoke English.

During practice, oddly enough, these language barriers weren't that formidable. I was able to demonstrate what I wanted and, since much of the Chinese language is composed of pictures, a picture really was worth a thousand words. Also, the players all had their own interpreters and I managed to get my messages across.

The first hint of trouble came during our initial game when I called time-out. The players gathered around me and an army of interpreters gathered around them. "Well," I began ... Before I could continue, all the interpreters translated, "Well," into their own languages. The next voice I heard was that of the referee saying the time-out was over.

Somehow, the team played a little better after that and went on to win the game. A local journalist wrote that my ability to say the right thing at the right time had saved the day.

While I was waiting for the season to start, I was also beginning to learn a little about life in Italy. When I first arrived, I thought of myself as rather sophisticated, even cultured. I had gone to a major university in a great city, had done some travelling and met many different kinds of people. But Italy was an awakening to me. I found an elegance there, a joy in the simple art of conversation and a people determined to enjoy life to an extent that I had never encountered before. And I had the good luck to arrive there at the best possible time.

It was the period of the great boom in Italian filmmaking. The industry was going through a golden era, as Hollywood had three decades earlier, so Rome held a great attraction for people from all over the world. The Americans and the French and people from much of Europe descended on the city in great numbers; armies of pretty girls came to work in the movies. It was an exciting time and I had the great fortune to meet two Americans who acted as my guides to getting along in and enjoying the country.

One was Jack Geiger, an American journalist, who taught me to overlook such minor irritations as the Italian telephone system and the fact that commerce, Italian style, closed down during the afternoon siesta. He showed me how to appreciate the art and the food and the pace of the city. Through Jack, I met many people I might never have found on my own.

The other, who became my best friend during this period, was Harry Cushing, an American expatriate whose mother was a Vanderbilt and who had come to Europe to devote himself to polo and to produce an occasional film. Harry's wedding to an heiress to much of the Swift meatpacking fortune was one of the social events of one particular season. I thought it was touching when they gave each other matching Rolls Royces. Harry published a weekly paper for the American community and I promptly found myself the movie editor, which got me invited to all the film festivals and parties.

By Italian standards, my salary was quite high and I paid almost no taxes on it. I had the happy combination of money and time and I enjoyed them both to the fullest. I joined a sports club on the Tiber where I played volleyball and swam and a poker group presided over by Bruce Cabot, the American actor, where I met many more people.

I lived in a lovely apartment in Parioli, the most exclusive part of town, and there always seemed to be a party going on. During one of them, everyone was gathered around a buffet table in a very long room, when all of a sudden the room shifted as if it were a teeter-totter. As if on signal, all the men had moved to the other end. I looked up and saw that Anita Ekberg, then at the height of her popularity, had just walked in. She was immediately surrounded by an army of males and the buffet table was left to the women.

During this period, I began to comprehend the differences between the way basketball is organized in Italy and in the United States. Many of them arise from the way basketball took hold abroad and the fact that its development in Europe was really rather slow. After the YMCA—under R. W. Jones' leadership—got the game started, American soldiers furthered its spread during World War I. The adoption of basketball as an Olympic sport in 1936 added to its popularity, but it was not until the second world war that the sport really began to get off the ground. A large number of American troops were stationed in Trieste, which became the center of Italian basketball, supplying most of the country's best players for years. Livorno, army supply headquarters in the postwar years, became another big basketball town.

Even then, the game did not really begin to break through until it had developed locally. People had to learn it, figure out the strategy and see it on television before it could become truly popular. Then, as club teams began to develop in the small towns, the Italian federation wisely adopted the same play-off and championship formula that was so successful in soccer; the competitive aspect added to basketball's growth.

To understand this, you must know a few basic details about the organization of sports in Europe. In the United States, with the exception of the professional leagues, sports are arranged horizontally. One large body—usually representing the schools—runs the programs of many sports and that body's officials are responsible for all of them.

In Europe, and in most of the rest of the world, sports are set up vertically; each one is organized from top to bottom by a federation responsible only for that sport. Each federation is concerned with its particular sport on every level, from pre-teenage to the Olympics. The best way to visualize this is to think of American professional baseball several decades ago. Each major-league team contained, in its system, a whole network of minor-league teams of players with varying abilities. The Triple A team was at the top of the minor-league system, which descended through Double A to A, B, C and D.

European sports are set up in this way. There is a major league—which is called the first division—a second division, a third division and usually a fourth. And the Europeans have added to this a system of changing divisions, which makes for a great deal of fan interest. Each year, the two teams in the first division with the poorest records are dropped to the second division and replaced by the two second-division teams with the best records. This heightens incentive in the lower ranks of the first division where the struggle to avoid being dropped into the second division can be intense.

Generally, first-division teams represent the cities with the bigger arenas. Salaries are higher in the first divisions and vary from country to country, with Italy, France, Belgium and Spain generally paying the most money. Even within a division, the range can be great. The top clubs with winning traditions to maintain— Real Madrid in Spain, Standard Liege in Belgium, Ignis Varese in Italy and a few others—may pay twice as much to a few select players as other first-division teams pay their best players. As a result, these top clubs dominate their leagues the way the New York Yankees of old did.

Another extremely important factor in the development of sports in Italy in the last twenty-five years is the national soccer lottery. The amount of money that is bet is so large that the proceeds have paid for the construction of modern facilities all over the country, without the government contributing a dime. Much of this money has been plowed into the country's basketball program. As a result there are fine new arenas everywhere and the financing of the Italian national team is on a solid footing.

I have often thought that the Italian-style lottery could be adopted easily in the United States. By introducing a system of betting on professional baseball, football, basketball and so on, we could solve the financial problems that amateur sports face constantly. The puritans, in sport and out, would be terribly offended, of course, and call it another step on the road to hell. And the officials of the various sports would predict fixes and the destruction of their games' integrity. Organized crime, which makes billions each year on illegal betting in the United States, would also be bitterly opposed.

The truth is that a lottery can be easily, cheaply and honestly run and would provide vast sums of money that could be used to develop the facilities we so badly need and mass participation in sports of all kinds. We could build national sports centers where we could train our best athletes for international competition. We could take giant strides toward improving our teams in all sports, including those to which we pay little attention today. Along with track and field, swimming and basketball—sports in which we are already proficient—we could develop world-class archers, cross-country skiers, fencers and so on.

In addition, lottery money could be used on the local level to encourage sports in the neighborhoods. High schools could shore up athletic programs, constantly threatened by lack of funds. The YMCAs could share in the proceeds, along with various athletic clubs. Neighborhood tournaments could be organized, the winners moving on to regional competition and, ultimately, to statewide and nationwide events. Development of championship-caliber players would accompany a broadening base of sports activity in the country.

Sketched out briefly, a blueprint like this may sound grandiose and utopian, yet it is exactly the sort of system that has led to the mass sports-participation boom in many countries around the world. Considering our resources that are just waiting to be tapped, it would be even easier for us if we had the will.

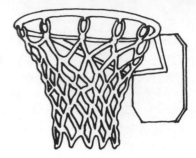

CHAPTER **4**

"Italy Wins, I Win"

ONE DAY, after I had almost forgotten what I had come to Italy for, the phone rang. It was the general secretary of the national basketball federation.

"We play France in two weeks at Trieste," he said. "Get your team together."

I had seen enough of Italian basketball by then to come to one important conclusion: the players on the national team, those with the biggest reputations, were not the players I wanted. They seemed slow to me and thoroughly indoctrinated in a static, controlled type of game I wanted to get away from. But I had seen younger players with possibilities on various club teams around the country. I invited the best of them to join the team, ignoring virtually everyone who had been on it the year before. This caused quite a stir and soon everybody was watching to see whether or not the crazy new American coach knew what he was doing. I was like an incoming president of the United States during the honeymoon period; judgment was suspended while I got my chance.

The players were basically the sons of the middle and upper classes and most of them had attended college. This was typical of the way basketball had developed in many countries. Soccer is the game played by the masses; basketball takes hold on the higher social and economic levels, then works its way down.

As soon as the team was assembled, I did three things unheard-of at the time in European basketball. First, I made the players run. I told them I wanted a team going full speed every moment it was on the court. Instead of the half-court practices they were used to, with everything carefully diagrammed and planned, I had them fast-breaking and free-lancing, taking advantage of situations as they occurred without worrying about set plays.

Next, I instituted the full-court press which was unknown in Europe at the time and created an immediate sensation. Defenses were as slow and static as the offenses and the concept of every man being constantly guarded all over the court was radical beyond belief.

The last innovation was the platoon. None of the players could go at full speed the way I demanded for the entire game so I substituted freely. I called the second team, a small, speedy bunch, my "dynamites," which came out "dee-na-*mee*-tees" in Italian. They were my shock troops who ran and ran and ran some more while the first-stringers rested. They quickly became some of the most popular players on the team among the fans.

All of this strategy was common to basketball in the United States at the time. The European game was easily twenty years behind. Much of the play revolved around a big, slow center and action moved deliberately, almost ponderously, as the plays were set up. The jump shot had just been introduced and was in its most primitive stages; the game was played with a great deal of grappling and manhandling, so that at times it almost resembled rugby. I was determined to change it.

Our first game in Trieste attracted a great deal of attention. There were at least 6,000 people in the arena, eager to see how the new team would do against one of the traditional powers of European basketball. France had been the top Western European team in the 1952 Olympics in Helsinki and usually ranked among the highest finishers in the European championships. But the

French players had no idea how to cope with the press or our breakaway tactics and we beat them, 64–56. It was the first postwar win for Italy over France and when it was over the fans rushed out onto the floor, hugging and kissing us all. They were delighted not only by the victory but also by our exciting style of play.

Style, I soon learned, is almost as important as results to the Italians. They love nothing so much as action taken with great enthusiasm and daring. Coaches, on the other hand, had to remain utterly calm and collected. You seldom saw Italian coaches chewing towels or jumping off the bench and screaming at the referees. If you did not react quickly, you gave the impression you were very wise and having profound thoughts while everybody around you— player and fan alike—was wildly excitable. Such behavior was totally foreign to me, but I found a way to accomplish it. Before every game, I took tranquilizers. Sure enough, somebody would occasionally write approvingly in the press, "McGregor showed himself not only to have nerves of steel because he didn't get excited when the referees' calls went bad, but remained composed when the game wasn't going well." Today, this has all changed. Coaches in Europe rant and rave just like those in America.

After our opening success in Trieste, we went on to other big moments, building up a strong record against the national teams of other countries. Our first major international tournament was the Mediterranean championships in Barcelona, where we came in second to Spain. The most amazing thing about the title game was that it was ever finished. There were 10,000 people in the arena and they were all going crazy. But what really caused problems was that most of the fans had brought whistles with them. It was impossible to tell which whistles belonged to the referees and which did not. The only way they could stop the game was by intercepting passes.

Late in the game, with the score very close, a referee stepped in front of a pass, ran over to the scoring table, slapped his hand down and shouted, "The last five baskets don't count!" Four of them were ours and Spain was soon the Mediterranean champion.

Everywhere the team went in Italy for the next few years, it was the object of great attention and excitement. In 1954, we played a game in Naples against Bulgaria and had an excellent night. The Neopolitans turned out to be among the most enthusiastic fans in all of Italy and they seemed to respond to the team's fast play even more warmly than usual. On leaving the arena after the victory, I was approached by a little guy who said, in an accent that surprised me because it was right out of Brooklyn, "Nice going, kid." And he handed me an envelope. I put it in my jacket pocket and forgot about it. Days later, I came across the envelope and opened it. Inside were two $100 bills and a note. "Italy wins, I win," it read. It was signed by Lucky Luciano. I wonder what would have happened if we had lost.

One thing I had a hard time getting used to was the Italian tendency to let everything wait until the last minute. We were always waiting for transportation, waiting for schedules to be arranged, waiting for equipment. The fact that somehow things always worked out didn't make the waiting any easier.

Once, scheduled for a nationally televised game against Bulgaria, we were sitting in our locker room waiting for our uniforms to arrive. The appointed hour grew closer and closer and there was the Italian national team in its jockstraps. I wanted to give the coach's classic pep talk: "Go on out there and knock them dead." With five minutes to go, the uniforms arrived and the Italian public was spared a spectacle it might never have forgotten.

The success of the team made me something of a celebrity among the Italians. I began to be recognized by service-station operators and mailmen and to learn the truth of the theory that it is often easier to make a name for yourself in a foreign country than in your hometown. One night, Harry Cushing and I were having dinner at the Grand Hotel in Rome when Gary Cooper, who was there making a movie, walked by and stopped to visit with Harry. Just then, a young boy walked up and asked for an autograph. Cooper turned and reached for the piece of paper when the boy said, "Not you, sir. I would like Coach McGregor's autograph."

The combination of my new game and my society friends brought me another novel asset—easy introductions to a wide variety of women. My wife and I had split permanently by then, and I reacted in about the way you would expect of a boy from Portland, Oregon, who had been plopped down magically in one of the world's most romantic cities. I went wild. I had a lot to learn, though, the most important lesson being to forget about the Italian girls altogether. They were lovely to look at and happy to be pursued, but only if marriage was on your mind. There was, I discovered quickly, no such thing as a casual romance. They had courtships that lasted longer than my marriages did.

Happily for me, however, beautiful girls from Scandinavia, Germany, Britain and the United States were flocking to Italy by the tens of thousands. Usually, they were snapped up by Italian men, but after a while, finding their Italian courtiers jealous and possessive, they gravitated into our circle. It was not long before I was running what amounted to a boarding house for women from other countries. It was not unusual for three or four of them to be staying in my apartment at the same time. In the course of a year, there might be as many as thirty in and out. I had a tremendous place, a penthouse with a big terrace, three bedrooms and a living room. There was a restaurant below where we could eat or have food sent up. It was a perfect arrangement.

I soon discovered that the best way to meet girls was through other girls. They were the greatest bird dogs of all. Once, several of us ran into a sculptress who was having a hard time financially and we struck a deal. We found her an apartment and paid her rent and she introduced us to her models as patrons of the arts. Every two or three weeks, she would come wandering by with another gorgeous girl in tow.

Then, too, Harry Cushing was a great one for throwing parties. He had what he called a permanent floating cocktail party and there was always a group of us on call. He would meet a new girl and say, "I'd like you to be the guest of honor at a cocktail party

I'm throwing." Actually, the party did not exist until that moment. He would make a few calls, and, *voilà*, instant party. His chauffeured Rolls would pick up the new girl and she would arrive, never knowing that she was the reason for the party.

Long ago, my mother had taught me you had to die before you could go to heaven. During my first few years in Italy, I began to have my doubts.

CHAPTER **5**

The Road to Budapest

IN THE SPRING of 1956, the Italian national team travelled to Hungary for the European championships. It was my first experience as coach in a major international event as well as my first trip to Eastern Europe and I looked forward to it with great anticipation. Italy had never done well in this tournament, but I was pleased with the progress of the team and confident we would finish high in the twenty-two nation field.

To the Hungarians, however, the championships meant a great deal more. It was the first time in a long while that any sports delegations from the West had competed in their country and they were eager to play host. We could see this was to be no ordinary trip the moment we began the train ride from Vienna to Budapest. Even though we had an official from the Hungarian basketball federation riding with us, our luggage, passports and train compartments were checked four times during the two-hour trip. And when we arrived at the Hungarian border, we were stopped for another inspection that lasted for an hour and a half. Finally, they were ready to let the team enter, but with one exception. Me.

I was undoubtedly the first non-government visitor with an American passport to appear in quite some time and it was clear they felt this required special consideration. I would have to remain behind while they decided what to do. But the players and the Italian officials held firm. If McGregor stays, we all stay, they said, and finally the Hungarian sports official, who seemed terribly embarrassed, managed to convince the border guards that it was all right. We entered Hungary.

From the first, the Italians were the hit of the tournament. The Hungarian people simply loved everything about them—from their fashionable tailor-made travelling outfits to the verve and excitement with which they played the game. I think the fact that Hungary was a Catholic country, where religion was tightly controlled by the government, had something to do with the way the people reacted to the representatives of another Catholic country. Also, I believe Italy represented a whole way of life that had been lost to them: the music, the fashion, the elegance and the style. And the players, good Italians all, responded in kind. On the street, they made a great show of friendship wherever they went; on the court, they threw flowers and blew kisses to the crowds. The Italians loved every minute of it.

Most of all, they loved the girls. In later years, I would see groupies following players around and making a fuss over them, but to this day I have never seen anything to equal the way the Hungarian girls reacted to the Italian players. Upon learning who they were, the girls would walk up to the players on the street and smother them with kisses. The girls all seemed incredibly beautiful and able to make themselves chic using nothing more than burlap sacks. The fact that few of the girls spoke Italian and none of the players spoke Hungarian didn't stop them. They communicated through song and through making love. There was a vast amount of both while we were in Hungary.

The team was assigned an interpreter who was with us constantly and a few of the Hungarian players let it be known that he was with the secret police. He tried to ingratiate himself and every so often asked if we were interested in black-market goods. Having been warned, we were careful to talk and act discreetly while he was around.

The tournament itself was played in an outdoor soccer stadium and the games regularly drew crowds of 50,000 or more. I was amused at the way the Hungarians handled the parking situation. The stadium would be filled to capacity but since the average fan couldn't afford a car, there would be only half a dozen official limousines parked outside along with the chartered buses that had brought the teams.

We had a couple of easy early games and, inspired by the fact that there were at least 500 Hungarian girls in our reserved rooting section, we won handily. One of the attitudes that surprised me was the graciousness of the fans to all the visiting teams. They cheered hardest for their own team, of course, but even the Russians, who were not exactly loved, were greeted with polite applause. The Hungarians seemed anxious to show what good sportsmen they were.

There was only one occasion when they let their true feelings get the best of them. In a game between two Eastern European countries, the crowd went almost berserk at every call of a Belgian referee. Spectators booed and shook their fists and yelled what must have been choice Hungarian curses. The hysteria reached such a point that the police began removing people from the arena. I couldn't understand it so I turned to our interpreter and said, "For God's sake, what's going on?"

"Can't you see?" he shouted over the noise. "That man looks exactly like Khrushchev."

Apparently, the Hungarians saw the resemblance as a chance to show their Western visitors what they thought of any and all things Russian.

After our strong early start, we ended by losing to the Soviet Union, Hungary and Czechoslovakia, which finished first, second and third in the tournament. The loss to the Russians, who were the defending champions, was particularly difficult to take since we were ahead by a point with very little time left when one of our top players fouled out. I took his substitute aside, warning him that the Russians were certain to run a play at him and that he should watch out for the fake-and-drive that was such an integral part of their attack.

The Russians threw the ball in. The player who got it headed straight at our new man and gave him a head fake. Our man promptly became the first astronaut and the Russian simply waited until he was safely out of the way before going in for the winning layup.

That defeat left us with one game to play, against Yugoslavia for fifth place in the tournament. A victory would still be a great achievement; Italy had never finished higher than thirteenth in the tournament and Yugoslavia was then the slumbering giant of European basketball, just about to achieve the power that would soon make it a dominant force on the continent. Thus, the contest was important to the sports ambitions of both countries.

The game was played at night, which meant the evening dew would be a factor, and when it began, the look on the face of the Yugoslavian coach matched my own. We were both panicked. The dew was far heavier than it had been on any previous night of the tournament, and both teams were slipping around on the floor so badly that it was clear the game would be won by the team with the most traction, not the most talent.

About ten minutes into the first half, the Yugoslavian coach called time-out. When I looked across the way, I saw him pouring onto the floor a foamy white substance that looked exactly like melted marshmallows. When I saw the Yugoslavian players stomping this stuff into their shoes, I knew exactly what its purpose was, even if I never did learn its identity. And it worked like magic. Suddenly, only we were slipping and sliding around on the floor and the Yugoslavians were off to a good-sized lead. Marshmallows, I kept saying to myself as we fell farther and farther behind. They're going to beat us with goddamn marshmallows. Why the hell don't we have some?

Then it hit me. We might not have any marshmallows, but we had something else that just might work. I shouted for a time-out. While the players were approaching the bench, I dug into one of our equipment bags for the boxes of raisins we carried for quick energy and poured out every one I could find onto the floor.

"Step on these," I said. "Grind them into your shoes."

The players looked at me as if they thought I was crazy, but it worked. They stopped skidding and we won the game by a point. It may not have been the best basketball ever played, but it certainly had to be the tastiest floor. At least on our side.

We were jubilant at our fifth-place finish—the best of any non-communist country in the tournament—which established Italy as a force to be reckoned with for the first time.

The scene at the Budapest train station as we prepared to leave looked like the troops going off to war. Hundreds of women were crying and hugging the Italian players and exchanging last-minute notes and photographs. A few girls even tried to climb into the players' duffle bags and smuggle themselves out. My mind, however, was on other things.

Once the word had gotten out that I was an American, I became one of the most sought-after men in Budapest. I wish I could say it was because of my good looks and worldly charm, but the truth was quite different. Just about everybody in Hungary, it seemed, had a relative or a friend in the United States they had not seen or heard from in years. The Hungarian players and coaches, in particular, asked me to send letters and notes and call people once I got back home. I could hardly refuse, but for days all I could think about was that inspection station at the border. It had been difficult enough getting into Hungary. I didn't want any trouble getting out.

As it happened, there was no trouble at all. We sailed through the border checkpoint and back into Austria with all the letters, notes and phone numbers safely intact—inside a couple of dozen basketballs, the old-style variety that had to be laced up after being inflated. It was a good thing none of the border guards thought of bouncing them.

There is a short postscript to this story. Not long after the tournament in Budapest, the Hungarian revolt broke out and was soon brutally put down by the Russians. A year or so later, we were playing a game in Vienna when I suddenly found myself staring into the face of the man who had been our interpreter in Budapest, the one we had been warned about.

"Do you remember me?" he asked.

"Yes," I said. "I'm surprised to see you here."

"I was a freedom fighter," he said. "I escaped as the revolution was being crushed."

I knew better. A Hungarian coach who had defected during the revolt warned me that what was not sufficiently understood by the Western world, which was so sympathetic to the hundreds of thousands of refugees, was the existence of *two* waves of people escaping the country. In the first were collaborators with the regime, afraid the revolution might succeed, and getting out to save their necks. The second wave was made up of people fleeing communism. Some of those who had left in the first wave were instructed to stay out to spy on the second group. The coach told me that our friend the translator was one of these.

About players and coaches defecting from Eastern Europe, I must, of necessity, be brief. I have helped about half a dozen such people get jobs in the West after they left their own countries. Some of them have had permission to leave. Yugoslavia, in particular, holds out the lure of playing in Italy or France to a player who has been on the national team and has reached the age of thirty-five or so. Coaches who have been around for a long time are often afforded the same privileges.

But those who want to defect are faced with a painful choice. If they leave their countries, they know they may never see their families again. Yet they never give up hope that one day they may be allowed to go back to visit or to bring their relatives out.

"For Christ's sake," one coach from Hungary said when I told him I was writing this book, "don't mention my name. For the first time in thirteen years, they're letting me back in to visit my parents."

CHAPTER **6**

Addio, La Dolce Vita

THE SCENE IN VENICE, where the team split up after returning from Hungary, was nearly as tumultuous as it had been at the other end in Budapest. The Italian fans were excited about our good showing in the tournament and the station was filled with flowers, shouts of joy and much kissing and hugging. I continued on to Rome where I found a welcoming party from the national basketball federation that swept me off to its headquarters for a reception. My stock in Italy had never been higher and I was convinced it would go on like that forever. It was not long, however, before disaster struck in an entirely unforeseen manner. The 1960 Olympics were awarded to Rome.

A tremendous outpouring of national pride greeted the announcement and the president of the basketball federation, Decio Scuri, proclaimed that the national team was ready to compete in the 1956 Olympics at Melbourne. I was pleased with this and looked forward to coaching in my first Olympics. We had an excellent, well-prepared team that had met top competition in the European championships and would, I was sure, do well in Australia. Then I learned that, in his enthusiasm, Scuri had overlooked the facts of life concerning Italian basketball.

Normally, the Olympics are held during the summer. But our summer is the Australian winter and the Melbourne Games were set for late November and early December. This was many weeks after the Italian club-team season had begun and the sponsors of those teams were businessmen first and foremost. They would no more consider postponing their season in deference to the Olympics than the National Basketball Association would in the United States. The owners announced that no club players would be available for the Italian national team during the Olympics. Since all of my best players came from the clubs, the team would be decimated.

Scuri was faced with an excruciating dilemma. There was no way he could back down from his promise of an Italian team at Melbourne without severe embarrassment, the worst fate that can befall a proud Italian. Yet he had no power to force or persuade the club owners to change their minds. In fact, he owed his position to them since the club teams elect the national federation officers. Scuri had to find a way out.

He made another announcement. A great tournament would be staged in Bologna during the first four days of September and the top eight teams in Europe would be invited. If Italy could repeat its performance in the European championships—that is, finish fifth or better—it would go to the Olympics. If not, it would remain at home. That was fine with me. I had no doubt that we would pass the test; in fact, the competition, so soon before the Olympics, would be beneficial to us. Then Scuri dropped a bomb. The national team, he said, would not be called together to practice until three days before the tournament.

"Three days!" I protested. "After a summer of inactivity? The other European teams will train for six weeks as part of their preparation for the Olympics. We're certain to lose."

"Those are the conditions," he said.

"I can't do that," I said. "I resign." And I stomped out of his office.

The next day, I received a call from the American Embassy in Rome. A first secretary asked me to come over to see him.

"We understand you want to renege on your contract with the Italian basketball federation," he said.

"They've made impossible conditions," I said.

"Mr. McGregor, you've become a personality in this country. You're a highly publicized symbol of America and it is important that we retain the goodwill of the Italians. I strongly recommend that you honor the terms of your contract."

He had me and he knew it. I was just getting started in international basketball and the goodwill of my government was critically important. If official word got out that I was an unreliable representative of the United States, it would be fatal. I went to Bologna.

The moment I arrived, I knew I had lost. First, it was hot as hell. Practice sessions would have to be kept short or the players, out of shape after a whole summer off, would be dying. Second, the gym we were assigned to practice in had no baskets. For two days, we would not be able to take a shot. The results were what I expected and what Scuri wanted. We didn't win a game.

"As much as we would like to send a team to the Olympics," Scuri announced with all the sadness he could muster, "it is obvious that our young team is simply not ready."

By losing, he had won. He had maneuvered the situation so that both he and the club team owners had ended up on the same side and he had saved face. I was the loser, of course, no longer the coach of the victorious Italian national team, but suddenly the coach of the team that could not qualify to go to the Olympics. Machiavelli would have been proud of Scuri that day. There remained only one thing for him to do. I had challenged his authority, and I had to go. There were still a few months remaining on my contract when he called me into his office.

"Jim," he said, "our personal relationship is not what it once was. We also feel that when we host the Olympic Games, the national team should have an Italian coach."

I could hardly quarrel with either statement, even though my assistant, the man who would take over as coach, had been born in Egypt and had not set foot in Italy until recently. Nevertheless, he was an Italian citizen.

"We would like you to finish out your contract with us by giving some clinics," Scuri said.

"Where do I go?" I asked.

"Elba."

Two days later, I took my Napoleon complex to the one place in Italy where there is virtually no basketball, not a single club team. I conducted an occasional clinic for high-school coaches and reflected on the ways of the American innocent abroad and how helpless he can be when faced with a centuries-old tradition of political brilliance. When I returned to Rome, Scuri had one last surprise for me.

"I like you, Jim," he said. "You've done a lot for basketball in Italy and I'm sure you'll be back one day. Instead of the ticket back to Portland that you're entitled to, I want to give you this."

It was a ticket for a trip around the world that included Australia, where I attended the Olympics without my team and saw France, a team we had beaten twice that year, place fourth.

CHAPTER 7

Kiev Nights

I HAD VERY LITTLE TROUBLE finding ways to keep busy for the next few years. My success in Italy led to offers from several countries, both to coach their national teams and to give clinics. The first job I took was as coach of the Greek team. When I arrived, the club was ready to begin training for an important home game against Poland; I could see the task would be formidable.

Poland had a very strong team and, as soon as I got a look at Greece's players, I thought we were in over our heads. I was afraid of becoming the first Greek coach to lose at home since the guy who handled Athens against Sparta. The team had some talent, but not a lot of depth and there was not much time to practice. But what I couldn't understand was why nobody else seemed to be worried—not the president of the Greek federation or the press or any of the players.

The game was played in the Olympic Stadium and the federation president approached me a short time before. I was expecting him to tell me how important the game was for the prestige of the country and how hard we must try to win. Instead, all he said was, "Defend the south goal and be ready to start the game on time." It was the strangest pre-game pep talk I had ever heard.

40

The start of the game was set for precisely 3:22 P.M. I have had teams in games that have started at all sorts of hours in my time, but never precisely at 3:22 P.M. I was soon to learn why. We began our warm-ups under the north basket, signifying this was the one we would shoot at during the first half. We would, as instructed, defend the south goal.

At exactly 3:22 P.M., the ball was thrown up at center court. And at exactly 3:22 P.M., the sun appeared over the rim of the stadium and shone directly into the eyes of the Polish players. They played .the entire first half totally blind, unable to see a thing on offense or defense. We ran up a twenty-point halftime lead.

I was still worried. We would have to switch baskets in the second half and then the sun would be in our eyes. Wrong again. As soon as the second half began, the sun dropped down gracefully over the edge of the stadium and the normal afternoon wind replaced it. The poor Poles ran into a headwind during the entire second half. They would throw a pass and the ball would blow back in their faces or out-of-bounds. All we had to do was play carefully, protect our lead and we had an easy victory.

After the game, I could hardly look the Polish coach in the eye. Blinded by the sun and chapped by the wind, he had just lost a fixed game. Fixed by nature.

A sequel to this story took place ten years later when I took a touring team to Greece for a game in the same stadium. I knew we wouldn't have a chance if it were played in the afternoon, so I insisted that it be scheduled at night. We ran up a big, first-half lead, but once again the Greeks outsmarted their visitors. At half-time, they put us in a locker room that was literally freezing. When we came out for the second half, we were as stiff as boards and never did thaw out entirely. The Greek team ran all over us and went on to an easy victory.

During my time as coach of the Greek team, I was asked to give a clinic in Poland. The State Department approved—a necessity in that heyday of McCarthyism—and I became the first American coach to go to any Eastern European country on his own since the end of World War II. It was an exciting prospect, so exciting that I didn't bother to consider what the weather would be like in Warsaw in January. It didn't take long before I realized my mistake.

I stayed at the Bristol Hotel, the best in town at the time, a distinction that didn't include central heating. Huge drapes hung at the entrance, so you went through a revolving door, then fought your way through a tent of fabric. Even then, the cold just crawled into you. I could never stop freezing. I was going for the world record for length of time sitting in a hot bath when my hosts came to take me to the clinic. It was held at the Palace of Culture, an architectural monstrosity that the Poles hated unanimously, as much for the fact that it was built by the Russians as for its ugliness. It, too, was unheated.

My whole clinic that day was given over to drills involving the maximum amount of footwork. I figured the Poles would benefit from this, but my primary objective was to keep warm. The whole routine soon turned into more of a song-and-dance performance than a basketball clinic.

"Move those feet!" I shouted as I whirled back and forth on the court. "Shift those hands!" And all the time I kept waving and dancing around. A lot of teams use warm-up drills like this, but none are quite as frenetic as those I demonstrated that day.

Years later, I returned to Poland—in the summer, of course—and visited a basketball training camp. And by God, there they were, going full speed through those same footwork and arm drills I had taught them just so I could keep warm.

While I was in Poland, I became intrigued with the possibility of going to the Soviet Union. There was very little exchange of tourists and no formal cultural or sports ties between the Russians and the Americans at the time, so I had no idea whether such a trip was feasible. But in 1958, the opportunity came.

I was attending a coaches' meeting in Finland and mentioned

to a Russian coach that I would be returning to Greece and would like to travel back through his country, giving some clinics there if it could be arranged. The approval process was painfully slow, but just as our meeting was winding up, the Russian coach told me that the trip had been approved. I was to give some clinics in Moscow and a few others in Kiev.

The clinics were extremely well organized. In Moscow, there was a genial reception and my remarks were tape-recorded. I had a battery of microphones in front of me and felt like Frank Sinatra. In both Moscow and Kiev, coaches had been brought in from all over the area and interpreters who knew something about basketball were provided. There must have been about seventy-five people at each session, asking penetrating, specific questions.

The Russians are, I think, the most avid students of the game in the world. They record, study and analyze everything about basketball they find. They film all of their best teams and their most important games. It was clear to me, from having watched them in international tournaments, that they had developed a national system or style of play to which every coach and player had to conform. Everything was done according to a preconceived plan. Even the fast break was choreographed to the most minute degree and nobody ever did anything on his own. When you became open for a shot, it was a result of the strategy of the play.

During the clinics, I tried to deal with this to some degree, remarking that in the United States we didn't have what amounted to a party line (I restrained myself from using those exact words) concerning strategy and techniques imposed from the top. With hundreds of colleges and thousands of high schools playing the game, and with each using its own tactics, it was simply impossible. I tried to get across the notion that our system might have some advantages because new tactics can develop from it.

Basketball in the Soviet Union was really quite primitive then. The players and the style of the game reminded me of how they used to describe the Chicago Bears—the Monsters of the Midway.

It was three yards and a cloud of dust. Offensive charging was a completely foreign concept to the Russians and their way of getting the ball down the court was to use a flying wedge, with blockers clearing the way for the man with the ball and almost knocking people down so he could force up a shot. Weight was an important factor in playing that kind of game.

Over the years, Russian basketball has evolved into a style similar to ours. I think their exposure in international tournaments to teams with more finesse has had a lot to do with this. In the 1972 Olympics, this evolution became complete with the arrival of Aleksander Beloff, the first Soviet star who played his own game. Beloff was the Soviet Jerry West, fast enough and slick enough to work his defender one-on-one. He was the first player the Russians ever allowed to work himself open and put up a shot.

Before the clinics in Kiev, I walked through some of the city, enjoying the parks and noticing that the people seemed more relaxed and open than they had in Moscow. I had a sense of euphoria over the fact that I was in a place where nobody I knew had ever set foot and that things were going so well.

I also did some shopping, although you actually sold more than you bought in the Soviet Union in those days. The black market for Western goods was brisk everywhere. My coaching colleagues freely admitted that the authorities never seemed to move against it unless upset about something else. Whenever they wanted to pick up somebody for an offense, particularly a political one, it was always safe to accuse the offender of dealing in illegal goods; virtually everyone who travelled did so. It was one of the holds they had on people.

I had made my preparations by stocking up on clothes, cosmetics and jazz records that I'd heard were popular: Count Basie, Benny Goodman and the like. Almost as an afterthought, it occurred to me to bring in several pairs of basketball shoes as well. Once I was in the Soviet Union, I realized I had no idea how to go about letting it be known I had items I was willing to sell. I did not think the authorities would take kindly to my setting up a stand on a street corner, nor did I know how to take out an ad in *Pravda* so I was in a bit of a quandary. It didn't take long before the problem was solved.

I had only to walk down the streets of Kiev and I would be approached by a Russian man who would point to my tie or my shirt or my wash-and-wear suit and smile. I had learned a few words of Russian—enough to establish a basic business relationship—and after a while my hotel room became a bargain-basement discount store. The clothes and the records went very fast, but the basketball shoes turned out to be my hottest item. They were all gone within hours. In a few days, I was swimming in rubles. Late one night, back in my hotel room after a post-clinic, vodka-drinking session with several Soviet coaches and interpreters, I decided to count up all the money and try to figure out what to do with it. There were stacks of rubles all over my bed when all of a sudden I heard BAM! BAM! BAM! at the door.

My heart began to pound—I was sure the police had come to haul me off for illegal currency possession or speculation in the black market—and I started shoving the money under the pillow and into my sweat pants, stalling for time by calling, "One moment," in as many languages as I could think of.

Finally, I opened the door and was astonished to confront the biggest, blondest woman I had ever seen. For a moment, I thought there might be two of her. She had to be six feet one or two, and close to 200 pounds, but on her it all looked good; she was absolutely beautiful.

"Who are you?" I finally managed to blurt out.

Her answer in Russian meant as little to me as the question in English had to her. I tried German and her face lit up. We were in business.

"I am Coach Seminoff," she said. "I couldn't come to the clinic this evening. Would you be so kind as to let me in?"

I tried to play it light, saying it would be a lot easier for her to get in than out.

Her response to that was, "I would certainly be grateful if you would review some of the things you said at the clinic."

I have a long record of not turning blondes away from my door after midnight, so in she came. For the first time, I noticed she was carrying a notebook and a sack. She sat down on the bed, reached in the bag and pulled out a bottle of vodka.

"You like drinks," she said. "It's chilly and vodka is warming."

It was cold in the unheated room, all right, and I certainly wasn't against warming up either one of us. She poured us both a drink, saying, "Here's a toast to Soviet-American friendship."

We talked about the fast break for a while and drank a toast to basketball. We talked about the high-low post offense and drank a toast to Naismith. We talked about Pete Newell's California defense and drank a toast to good old Pete. Pretty soon, we had toasted the glories of sport, the beauties of Kiev and each other. I wasn't actually drinking much of the vodka, but she was pouring it down as fast as she was taking notes and I was getting woozy on just the fumes.

After the long clinic, I had had about as much basketball as I could handle, but I kept going, hoping something on a more personal level would develop. I was still freezing and I threw a blanket over my shoulders, but, after six or eight rounds, she tossed off her coat. This allowed a closer inspection of her, prompting me to suggest we get those basketballs out of her blouse and try some ball-handling drills. But every time I went into my double-pivot offense, she deflected me easily.

The shuffle offense was a big thing in those days and she was quite interested in this. "Der shoofle," she said, after we had drunk a toast to the Olympic Games, so I found myself trying to explain this fairly elaborate system, wondering if we would ever leave basketball behind us for the remainder of the night. Soon, she was quite drunk and I was about to pass out from the vodka fumes. At about 2:30, I decided to try the direct approach.

"God, it's cold," I said. "Let's go to bed."

Her answer—I will never forget this—was, "But in bed, it's very hard to play basketball or drink." Now, how could you argue with that?

At one point, I just grabbed her and she said, "What are you doing?"

"I thought we might demonstrate overguarding from the front," I said, still trying to laugh it up. But through it all, I am convinced she never really appreciated my intentions.

Finally, I decided the hell with it. I would make sure there was no way she could mistake what I had in mind.

"It's late," I said. "Would you like to stay and sleep with me?"

"Oh, no," she said, "but would you like to come to my house?"

My God, maybe I'm in after all, I told myself.

"I sure would," I said.

So we drank a toast to the taxis of Kiev and set off to find one. Now the thing about Russian cabs is that people often make love in them because apartments are so crowded—two and three generations often live in just a few rooms—and hotels are expensive. Couples will hire a cab and give the driver a few rubles to go into a bar in order to have the car to themselves.

As a result, almost every Russian cab reeks of intimate physical activity. Unfortunately, Coach Seminoff was so big there wasn't much room to maneuver. I kept trying to grab her and nuzzle around a little, but she kept escaping.

With the sexual revolution, there isn't as much confusion anymore, but in those days the situation was vaguer. Yes could mean no, no could mean maybe, and just because a woman was pushing you away didn't mean you should stop trying. Add to this our language problem and I still had room for hope.

Near the end of the ride, I grabbed one huge thigh, but she pulled away and said, "One moment, we'll be home quickly."

That did it. I was sure I was in. But when we reached her place, I got the shock of my life. It was like opening a phone booth and having ten college students fall out on you. I thought I had stepped into the stateroom scene in *A Night at the Opera*. It was four in the morning and there were people all over the place. I could not have demonstrated the jump ball.

Coach Seminoff introduced me all around as her American friend which led to more toasts. Admitting defeat, I said I had better get home so she called a cab. It was hard to get one at that time of night—they were all in use by people doing what I wished

I was doing—so I sniffed some more vodka and tried to keep from falling asleep.

Finally, a cab came. She took me outside and said, "Thank you very much. It's been wonderful," kissing me on the cheek. The cab driver, half-drunk, turned to me and said, "Amerikanish, great." He reached into a sack and pulled out a bottle of vodka. He weaved all over the road back to the hotel, proposing toasts to Soviet-American friendship.

Late the next morning, I woke up with the groggy realization that I had one more day to figure out what to do with all my rubles. It was illegal to take them out of the country and they couldn't be converted into Western currency. I had already bought a beautifully crafted ivory chess set and a couple of nice cameras, but I didn't see anything else I really wanted.

I had a vague idea of buying transportation. I looked into the possibility of returning to Russia some day and travelling back to the United States through Siberia. But it didn't seem practical at the time so there I was, ready to leave the Soviet Union with a large amount of rubles to dispose of. After my last clinic in Kiev, I mentioned my problem to one of the coaches as we sat in a bar. He spoke some German and we had become friendly.

"How about a holiday?" he asked. "You could fly down to the Black Sea."

"No, I've got to leave," I said. "I just don't see what the hell I can do with this money."

We talked some more and, as the hour grew later and the string of empty vodka bottles grew longer, I finally said, "Look, I'll give you the money. Maybe sometime in the future I'll be back and there will be something I can buy."

He protested, but I reached into my pocket and handed over the money.

"This is enough to buy a car," he said.

"Great," I said, "buy yourself a car."

"Yes, I'll give them the money, get put on a list and in eighteen years a car will be delivered." We both laughed.

In the end, he kept the money. We corresponded a few times and he assured me that any time I came back to Russia my rubles were waiting for me. But I never made it to Kiev again. I hope the money was of some use to him.

The question of what to do with Eastern European currency was one I would face constantly over the years. The money was useless outside the country that printed it and it was impossible to convert it. After a time, I learned to take my cut in trade. I would leave Czechoslovakia with wristwatches, Poland with crystal or silver, Hungary with fine china and so on. There were times when the teams I would shepherd to Eastern Europe resembled a group of travelling merchants rather than basketball players. Normally, this would have been illegal, but with the cooperation of the authorities, it couldn't have been easier. There was no way you could take these stunning crystal goblets, decanters, glasses and bowls out of, say, Poland, legally. But if you had a certificate from the Ministry of Sport, stating that they were trophies won in competition or gifts from the Polish people, it was suddenly all right.

On one trip to Poland, I received a gift that taxed my ingenuity to the utmost—half a carload of vodka. I didn't want to pay duty on it, so I had it shipped to a free-port warehouse in Rotterdam, where it sat for some time before I finally got rid of it. I had no wish to be in the vodka business—or the crystal, china, silver, camera or wristwatch business, either. I kept a few of the items I really liked for myself and then began looking for a way to unload the rest.

I discovered all sorts of entrepreneurs ready to help me out. Vienna, in particular, seemed to be loaded with people who did millions of dollars worth of barter business. It was no trouble for one of them to take my insignificant half-carload of vodka and, for a fee, trade it to a fellow moving sporting goods that I could use. I got rid of a lot of my "gifts" and "trophies" that way.

Leaving the Soviet Union that first time, we flew from Kiev to Vienna when a bad storm forced us down on what looked like an old airfield. We were allowed out of the plane and the first thing I saw, quite a distance away, was what appeared to be rows and rows of windmills. I ran back to the plane, grabbed my binoculars and camera and saw that they were actually helicopters, hundreds of them, the biggest I had ever seen. I had been in Russia long enough to know that all the train stations and airports had signs identifying the city, but the space for the sign on the old airport building was blank. I took out my camera and started taking pictures of the helicopters. A mistake.

In a moment, I heard a loud chorus of *"Nyet! Nyet!"* and felt something sharp in my back. I turned and saw it was a bayonet.

The soldiers took away my camera and looked as if they would like nothing better than to take me away, too. But I pulled out my letter from the Soviet sports federation that said I was an official guest. That—and the fact that it had been a forced landing and I had hardly asked to be there—seemed to do the trick. After a few more angry looks, they let me back on the plane and we flew to Vienna.

It was hard to get out of my mind all those huge helicopters sitting on an isolated field somewhere in western Russia. Not long afterwards, I was in Paris and decided to go to the American Embassy. I told a receptionist I wanted to discuss a question of military intelligence with somebody official. After a short wait, I was sent to see a man who was identified only as Mr. White.

I told him the story, that we had been blown off course and landed somewhere about two-hours flying time from Vienna, and that I'd seen 200 large helicopters.

"That's interesting," he said. "I'm glad you came in. Tell me, are you ever likely to return to Russia?"

"It's possible," I said.

"Well, if you do go, please let me know. And if we don't contact you, I wonder if there is one thing you could bring us?"

"What's that?"

"A phone book. From any city. Just pack it up and bring it out."

I couldn't believe it. I had come in talking about a fleet of military helicopters and he was interested in phone books. Three months later, I got a letter at home in Italy. Inside were five $100 bills and a note that said, "Thanks. White." I never heard from him again.

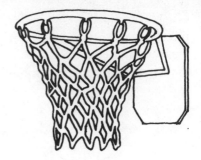

CHAPTER **8**

Walter Mitty and the Watusis

SHORTLY AFTER MY TRIP to the Soviet Union, the State Department asked me to give several clinics in Africa. I also received invitations from the federations of Mozambique and South Africa. I had never been to Africa and was happy to go for that reason alone, but I had another objective. I could hardly wait to get a look at the Watusis, those legendary, seven-foot giants with their amazing leaping ability. I saw myself becoming the Abe Saperstein of Africa, travelling the world with a team that would put the Harlem Globetrotters to shame.

But when I got to Bukavu, in what was then the Belgian Congo, I found that only a few Belgians played basketball. The Watusis were on what amounted to a reservation in Ruanda-Urundi, some two hours away. I commandeered a backboard, a basket and a truck and went to see them.

The Watusis lived in an area that resembled the Swiss Alps, not at all tropical in climate, but temperate and very beautiful. We drove to where they did a dance for tourists in a makeshift area roughly the size of a basketball court, with graduated seating made out of banks of earth on the sides. When I saw their tribal war dance, I was sure of one thing: If we could get them to do that during warm-ups, the other teams would run back to the dressing room.

I asked permission to put up the basket on the back of the truck and a lot of curious kids came out to see what we were doing. They were tall, all right, and graceful as could be, elegant in long gowns similar to the robes monks wear in Thailand. But as soon as we started throwing the ball around, I found the Watusis to be exactly the opposite of everything I had heard about them. Instead of being muscular, sinewy and athletic, they were almost painfully thin and fragile.

When we started demonstrating a couple of basic shooting drills, it was clear they would never be able to play the game well; they lacked stamina, strength and coordination. The tallest ones did learn a variation of the dunk shot, in which they just walked up to the basket, jumped a little way off the ground and dropped the ball through the hoop. Other than that, they couldn't shoot at all or handle the ball. Even their jumping ability turned out to be overrated. Those newsreel shots of Watusis leaping over high fences were rigged. They jumped from a step.

It was explained to me later that the basic problem was a long-standing social one, combined with inadequate diet throughout the years. The Watusis wandered into central Africa from the Sudan hundreds of years ago and, being so tall and graceful, they convinced people they were gods and should be treated as the ruling class. With this mystique going for them, they had to do very little actual work. Thus, they simply didn't develop any real physical skills to accompany their remarkable size.

Still, I thought the Watusis could be taught enough of the basics of basketball to set up a tour, but when I made inquiries I soon saw it would be impossible. I would need the permission of the colonial authorities for the Watusis to leave the country and the Belgians were very protective of them. This was brought home to me forcefully years later, after the Belgians had been expelled from the Congo and rival groups began settling old scores. War broke out between the Watusis and other tribes; the result was that these graceful, gentle people didn't have a chance and many were slaughtered.

When I arrived in Mozambique, I had a huge surprise waiting for me. For the first time in my life, I was a star. They were wild about basketball in this southeast African country—regularly drawing crowds of 10,000 or more to club games in the capital city of Lourenço Marques—but the quality of the sport there was very low. The only standard of comparison Mozambique had was with Portugal, whose colony it was at the time, and where its teams sometimes competed. But Portuguese basketball was far behind the rest of Europe, so the Mozambique players had never seen the game played well. The quality of play was about on a par with a low-level junior high school in the United States.

I had gone there as a coach, but as soon as I began putting on some shooting and dribbling demonstrations—my standard repertoire of pretty ordinary stuff—it became evident that, even at the age of thirty-seven, I was the greatest player they had ever seen. I was soon drafted to play for their various club teams and, all of a sudden, there I was, playing before large crowds, scoring more than thirty points a game. There were three games a week and I could hardly wait for the next one. Walter Mitty on his best day couldn't have dreamed up a situation like this.

In all the time I had played basketball, I had never been a star. In fact, it wasn't that often that I had been able to play. In the youth leagues of Portland and in high school, I was never more than a substitute. I was slow and short, without much spring, so I spent a great deal of time on the bench. I played fairly often only on my Boy Scout troop team. It was the weakest team in the weakest league in the city, but that didn't bother me. Unfortunately, this came to an end the night I got caught breaking into the gym we used for meetings in order to play basketball and was promptly kicked out of the Boy Scouts.

That left me only on teams where everybody else was better than I was and by then I was getting tired of sitting on the bench. So it occurred to me to form my own team. I went to the Broadway

Drug Store, conveniently located on the corner of my block, and asked the owner if he would like to sponsor a team. It would cost him only ten sweatshirts and a basketball. He went for it and, with my knowledge of the youthful basketball talent around town, I was able to put together a fairly decent team. The line-up changed constantly and we competed in several different leagues, but one thing remained the same: I played every minute of every game. Nobody could argue because we used my ball and my shirts. So there I was, at the age of twelve, locating a sponsor, looking for players and scheduling games. And here I am today, at the age of fifty-five, locating sponsors, looking for players and scheduling games.

Nor did my career pick up in high school. Jim Torson, the coach at Portland's Grant High, never cut me from the team, but he made very sure that my role never included much playing time. Torson liked me to help run the plays of our upcoming opponent in practice and to sit next to him on the bench during the games. He would then alternately discuss the progress of the game with me and direct loud complaints to the referees. Every so often he would get us mixed up and I would get yelled at while the referees would hear his discourses on strategy. On several occasions, I tried to sit down the bench from Torson, hoping he would put me in the game if I was not there as an audience. Each time he would yell, "Mac!" and I would tear off my warm-up jacket and head for the scorer's table to go into the game, only to be told to sit down in my usual place next to the coach.

Torson was responsible, however, for the small amount of glory I did attain as a high school athlete. It was his custom to make the players do a lot of distance running early in the practice season and often I won these races. In time, the track coach heard about this, and suddenly I was on the cross-country and track teams. By the time I graduated, I was state champion in cross country, city champion in the mile and still sitting next to Jim Torson during the basketball season.

Grant High had a fine track team; one of my better friends on the squad was Bob Likens who threw the javelin 212 feet, which

I think was a national high school record at the time. This caught the attention of Dean Cromwell, the famous track coach at the University of Southern California, who offered him a scholarship.

But Bob told him, "Well, I'm not too anxious to go down there. I don't know anybody. I think I'll probably go somewhere with Jim McGregor and these other guys I've been running with."

Suddenly, I found myself with a four-year track scholarship to USC, where I spent most of my time in the gym futilely trying to make the basketball team. In my senior year, my USC career came to an end when I went into the Marines, there to begin a stint that was unparalleled in its mediocrity, but which led indirectly to my last chance at collegiate athletic stardom.

I served my first few months as a Marine right on the USC campus, which was not exactly Tarawa. While most of my corpsmates were fighting far to the west of us in 1943, the Marines, in their infinite wisdom, moved me 3,000 miles to the east. I was assigned to a V-12 unit at Dartmouth and spent two years doing absolutely nothing worth mentioning.

The war had been over for a month or two when I was handling something heavy—I can't even remember what it was—hurt my back and received a medical discharge. I was out of the Marines some four months before the great mob of demobilized servicemen hit the job and college market. I figured that if I went back to USC, where my academic record was far from brilliant, I would get back into the social swing and might never graduate in time to find a decent job in competition with all those returning GIs. So, instead, I decided to go to the University of Minnesota.

I arrived there just as tryouts for the basketball team were beginning and, almost as a reflex action, I showed up for them. After a few days, the most amazing realization hit me. I was going to make the team because there was no competition. But, between the pre-registration period at the university and the final deadline for signing up for classes a week or so later, a couple of hundred thousand servicemen were released. All of a sudden, a six-year crop of high school basketball stars was fighting for spots on the team and I set the world record for downward mobility. In the space of a

day, I went from having a spot on the team to having difficulty
buying a ticket to the games.

I drowned my sorrows by going out for the swimming team and
actually winning a letter. For this, it was necessary only to score
a point in the dual meet with Wisconsin, Minnesota's traditional
rival. Luckily for me, Wisconsin had the weakest swimming team
in the Big Ten and I was able to chug in third in the 440 free-
style, thus scoring my lone point of the season.

After all these frustrations, you can imagine how I felt during
those two weeks as the toast of Mozambique. Finally, though,
the federation officials there asked me to go up to Beira, a city
many miles to the north, and put on a clinic. I bid a reluctant farewell to Lourenço Marques. On the way up to Beira, the train
stopped in a small town and I got off for a few minutes to stretch
my legs. I wandered into the fringes of the jungle, walked around
a bend in the path and in front of me I saw the end of my days
as a star. There was George King, who was a great player for the
Syracuse Nationals, an NBA All-Star and a brilliant showman.
He could do all the dribbling routines and shooting tricks with
which Pete Maravich and the Harlem Globetrotters have ever
excited a crowd.

I asked George what he was doing in the Mozambique jungle,
but I knew the answer. He was giving clinics, too. The moment
they got a look at what he could do with a basketball, there
wouldn't be a soul in the country who would remember my name.
I sent a letter of regret to the Mozambique federation and headed
straight for South Africa.

I've been to South Africa several times and I've always felt
welcome there. The national sports authorities invariably go out
of their way to make visiting coaches, players and officials comfortable. They are put up in the finest accommodations and their
every whim is fulfilled. It is obvious that the white South Africans
long for good will and respect more than anything in the world.
The country is very active in sports and extremely disturbed by the
isolation from international competition forced on it by official

apartheid policies. It is almost impossible to avoid political discussions, yet it is equally difficult to express any criticism of government policies when you are being treated so hospitably. Nor is it any easier when you find yourself on the other side of the fence, as I learned one day in Durban.

Some of the Zulus in that city hired themselves out to tourists, pulling them around in decorated carts very much like rickshaws. After I had been in South Africa for some time, I rode in one and began talking to the man pulling it. I was fascinated by his speech patterns—particularly by the clicking sounds that only the Zulus make—and enjoying the conversation when he asked me what I thought of South Africa.

"Well," I said, "I've seen quite a bit of Africa and what I'm going to tell you may or may not please you, but there's no doubt in my mind that material progress is greater here, for the whites and the blacks, than anywhere else. Most of the blacks I've seen here are better off than in other countries."

He didn't say anything for a moment and then I guess he decided he was going to be as frank as I had been.

"You goddamn American," he said. "You don't understand anything, you know."

"You asked me a question. I gave you an answer."

"I'm a Zulu. We're a fighting warrior tribe."

"Well, there hasn't been a hell of a lot of fighting down here. I don't see anybody revolting."

"There's a time to fight and a time to wait."

"That may be. I certainly hope something happens so it doesn't end up in mass bloodshed."

"Of course, you don't know what it's like to be completely in the power of somebody else, of another people."

"No, I don't. I guess it's terrible."

"But in a short time you're going to know exactly what it feels like to be in somebody else's power, the life-or-death power of somebody else."

"What do you mean, I'm going to be in that position?"

"You're in it right now."

He stopped pulling the cart and I saw for the first time that we were going up a steep hill.

"All I have to do," he said, "is let go of this thing and you're finished. How do you like it?"

I didn't like it at all. There was no way I could know if he was serious or not. It would have been the simplest thing in the world for him to let go and later say the rickshaw had slipped or he had fallen. He had made his point about living with your destiny controlled by somebody else and not being able to do a thing about it. He had made it very well, indeed.

After a moment, he started up again and we finished the rest of the trip in silence.

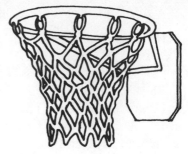

CHAPTER **9**

"I Think You've Got Cancer"

WHILE I WAS COACHING the Italian national team, we played Austria several times and I became friendly with some members of the basketball federation there. When they heard I was available, they asked me to coach the Austrian national team, and, in the fall of 1958, I was on my way.

Just before I left Italy, however, I noticed a strange swelling in one of my testicles and I thought I had better see a doctor. He took a look and grinned at me.

"Too much sex," he said, and he gave me some pills.

I drove off to spend a little time in the south of France before going to Austria, but my mind was not on my vacation. The swelling was getting worse, so I went to another doctor. He took a look and grinned, too.

"Not enough sex," he said, and he gave me some different pills.

I drove to Vienna. I had been on the job about three weeks when I was assigned to give a clinic in Graz, which is in the southern part of Austria, not far from Yugoslavia. The swelling had not gone down and after all that time I had begun to get nervous as well as uncomfortable. As I was driving past a building that said State Hospital, I stopped at the curb on an impulse, walked inside and asked to see a doctor. I was immediately shown into an office.

The doctor took a look and said, "I think you've got cancer."

A whirlwind of thoughts went through my mind. One was that this guy's bedside manner could stand some improvement; he certainly didn't use psychological preparation on his patients. Another was that I was going to be late for my clinic. And here I thought I was only going to get another knowing smile and a pill.

"What are you going to do?" I asked.

"First, I'm going to cut it off," he said.

"Both of them?" I said. There are very few soprano basketball coaches around, I thought. He ignored my remark.

"When will you operate?" I said.

"Today," he answered. "Now. I hope you haven't had lunch yet."

Within hours, I was in a hospital bed in Graz, Austria, minus one testicle. The tissue would have to be sent to Vienna for analysis before they would know whether or not I had cancer. It would take a couple of days for the report to arrive.

While waiting for the results of that test, I had two flashes. First, though I was in a ward with other cancer patients and I knew most of us would die, I was sure that I would not. People simply are incapable of accepting the imminence of their own deaths, no matter how close they might be to it, I decided. They always believe, with the certainty they believe anything, that they will be the ones to escape. It must be what soldiers feel in battle.

The other flash came just after I had been given a shot. I glanced up at the clock on the wall as the needle penetrated. The second hand had just reached twelve; it was exactly noon. I fell asleep and had a dream in which I relived the most remote periods of my life in the most intricate detail. Events I had forgotten years before were as vivid as the day they happened: going to school, my family, my travels, my coaching experiences. I woke up thinking it must be many hours later because of the nature and scope of my dream. It was twelve seconds past noon.

During the time I was waiting for the laboratory report, I asked one of the nurses about the doctor. I had just read about a man in the United States who had gone around pretending to be a doctor and I realized I had surrendered a testicle to a man about whom I knew nothing.

"Oh, Herr Doctor Professor," the nurse said. "He is the head of the hospital. A very great surgeon."

That made me feel a lot better. I asked her where he had practiced before coming to the hospital.

"On the Russian front," she said.

That explained his no-nonsense approach, at least.

Three days later, the doctor appeared in the ward with a huge grin on his face.

"I was right," he said. "It's cancer, a kind called seminoma."

I'm certainly glad to hear that, I thought. What would people think if they knew you were ever wrong?

"What do you do now?" I said.

"The lymph nodes come out."

"Holy God, that's a major operation."

"Yes, it is. It will take several hours."

"Why do you have to do that?"

"If the cancer has moved past the lymph glands, they will be swollen and we'll know that it is in other parts of the body. If the lymph glands are not swollen, we'll know that it hasn't and we can treat it."

The operation took five hours and I was a basket case for weeks afterward. I lost thirty pounds, was constantly doped up and barely conscious most of the time. Luckily, the lymph nodes had not been swollen so there was a pretty fair chance the doctors had gotten all the cancer, but I was to undergo treatment to make sure. For weeks, I had X-ray therapy that debilitated me even further, and my weight dropped to just under one hundred pounds. It was a long time before I felt any strength return. It got to the point where I began to measure what progress I was making not by whether I felt good but by whether I felt less bad than the day before. Any improvement, even of the smallest degree, was a cause for rejoicing.

The attitude of the nurses at the hospital was one of the few bright spots of my existence. They were Catholic nuns, many of them just girls, simple country people who cheerfully and with dedication worked long hours for other people for no salary at all. It was hard to keep from smiling when they were around. I learned my first new German word in the hospital from the nurse who came around every morning singing, *"einlauf, einlauf, einlauf."* She may have been the only person in the world who could make you smile at the thought of getting an enema.

I think I knew I was getting better when I started teasing one of the pretty young rosy-cheeked nuns about the two of us getting together.

"The Pope has thousands of nuns," I told her, "and I don't have anybody." The older nurses would also tease her about it and she would blush furiously.

I was never allowed to forget where I was, though. Everybody in the ward was a cancer patient and some of them died before our eyes. We would wake up in the morning and a bed would be empty. By the time I left, in fact, every person who had been in the ward when I arrived had been taken away in the night. Not a word was ever spoken about any of them.

Yet, for all this, there was virtually no complaining in the ward. Everybody seemed to do his suffering quietly. There was only one exception, a man who complained about everything. He complained about the food. He complained about the nurses. All day long, it was one thing or another. As I look back on it now, it is amazing how much we all came to hate that man. Somehow, we could live with the knowledge that we were terribly ill, but we could not accept any outward manifestation of it. Finally, the man's complaining got to the point that I decided to do something about it.

According to routine, when a patient died, a staff member would put a tag on his toe and a crew would come around at night and take him away. In the morning, that was how you found out who had died. In the middle of the night, I got up, took the tag off somebody who had died and slipped it on the toe of the complainer. In the morning, he was gone and he never returned. I consider that my greatest contribution to the ward.

In March, five months after I had entered the hospital, I was pronounced completely cured and told I could leave. I gave the doctors, the nurses and all the patients on the ward a confident farewell and walked out onto the street. The car that I had parked there the previous October was still there. Of course, the radiator had frozen and the battery was dead. Suddenly, after all that time in a cancer ward and after a close brush with death, it turned out that not being able to get my car started was the one blow for which I wasn't prepared. I realized that I had no money, no way to get anywhere, no place to go, really. I didn't feel so well any more, either. I sat in the car and cried.

After a long time, I went back into the hospital, utterly shaken. I took a lukewarm bath, feeling so weak it was hours before I could crawl out of the tub. After months of determination and the will to lick a dread disease, I felt defeated by the thought of facing the world.

In the end, it was the Austrian basketball federation that saved me. All the time I had been in the hospital, the federation had been a tower of strength, sending people to visit, paying my salary, telling me not to worry. But I hadn't been on the job long enough to acquire any insurance benefits so I still owed the hospital money and had no source of income. Once again, the Austrians came through. Several days after my collapse on the street outside the hospital, a federation official came by to say a new motor had been installed in the car and the organization was staking me to a long convalescent period at a mountain resort. Then he handed me an envelope, shook my hand and said goodbye. I was overwhelmed by this generosity and when I opened the envelope I began to weep again. It contained $1,000.

I stayed in the mountains for six weeks, enjoying the clean air and the scenery and regaining my strength. It was not long before

I began to wonder whether my illness and the loss of a testicle were going to affect my sexual appetite and ability. After a while, I began to brood about it. Then, one day, I got my answer.

The girl who made up the beds in the cabin was a big ripe German farm girl, really appealing if you are like me and not attracted by ninety-eight-pound models. One day, she came in while I was still in bed and I felt the first faint stirrings of an erection. There have been some great days in my life, but I want to tell you that one was tremendous. I had no idea whether I would be thrown into jail for what I was about to do, but on a day like that there was no help for it. I called her over.

"You know," I said, "I've been very ill. I've had a serious operation and I'm in doubt about whether I'll ever be able to perform as a man again."

She tittered a bit.

"It sure would be a wonderful thing," I said, "if you'd just jump into bed with me and warm me, let me see what happens."

I don't know whether it was my frail, 140 pounds that brought out the motherly instinct in her or my direct approach, but, as she giggled some more, she also undressed and climbed into bed. And that was how I worked my way back into the human race.

I returned to Vienna just in time to work the last few months of my contract and once again the Austrians were wonderfully kind. But it was clear that my contract was not going to be renewed and I could hardly blame them. They had gone to a lot of expense for a coach who had done them no good at all and they must surely have figured that I might die at any moment. So they gave me a few months' pay and I accepted a long-standing offer to go to Sweden.

CHAPTER **10**

Hello Sweden, Good-bye AAU

I BELIEVE that Sweden may well be my favorite place on the face of the earth. In the first place, it is obvious that somewhere in the middle of the country there is a huge lake into which they toss every woman unworthy of a Hollywood contract. Then there is the fact that making love has the same rating on the Swedish list of sins as taking a shower. And as lovely and liberal as the women are, that is how nice I have always found the people. I have coached there twice for extended periods and I always try to take my touring team there for at least a few days every year.

My greatest feat as a coach, in fact, is usually accomplished in Sweden. That is getting my players to leave. I often do this by saying we are taking a boat up to the northern part of the country where the girls are even more beautiful. The next morning, the players wake up in Germany and they don't speak to me for days. Needless to say, I prefer to end the tour in Sweden rather than start it there.

When I first arrived in Sweden in 1959, the quality of basketball was quite low. Hockey and handball were the two top sports and basketball was kept alive only by a few people who had attended school in the United States. But the Swedish federation adopted an intelligent tactic, which spread the sport widely through the country and which built its national teams to a respectable level. It taught basketball to the country's high school teachers. Along with coaching the national team, it was my duty to give clinics in the schools throughout Sweden. At one time or another, I must have appeared before every physical education instructor in the country. I had recovered my strength and I did a great deal of travelling to teach the game and its fundamentals.

Basketball in Sweden also got a break when a new school-building program was instituted and new gyms were required to be large enough to contain a court. Prior to that, gyms had been considerably smaller. Soon, the Swedes discovered that their height and coordination gave them a natural aptitude for the game and it began to spread.

In addition to teaching the teachers and coaching the men's national team, I was put in charge of a women's team. I cannot remember how we played, but I do know I set a record for substitutions. It has always been my habit to pat on the rear the player going into the game. Never had I coached players with such delightful rears and never did I do more patting.

It was during this period that I once again renewed my battle with the AAU. I was far from the only one fighting this petty, insulated organization at this time. For years, the AAU's control of U.S. participation in international sport had included a number of questionable bureaucratic techniques—such as the issuance of travel permits and licenses to play abroad—which put up barriers that stifled this country's participation against foreign teams. This time, my fight was no brief skirmish as it had been when I scheduled games for the Formosan and Philippine teams half a dozen years before. It was a lengthy, costly, all-out war of attrition that was not resolved for years. In a sense, it is still not over.

There are times when I look back and wonder what life would be like if there were no authorities to battle, no windmills at which to tilt. Quieter, probably, and certainly very different. My own war against the establishment began at the tender age of nine in Portland. It was then that I came up against one of the most enduring hazards the dedicated basketball player has to face: the locked gym.

I am a faithful reader of FBI crime statistics and, try as I may, I have never come across a single case of a stolen gym. Yet, in order to play when I was a kid—and to get in practice time as an adult—I have had to break into gyms all over the world. The first time I did this was at my own grade school, just three blocks from my house. It took little imagination and no tools. All we needed was something every kid had—bubble gum. We just jammed it into the lock socket so that it wouldn't close all the way and, presto, we could play any time we desired.

By the time I got to high school, sneaking into gyms had become a way of life. One day, the custodian gave me his gym key so I could do some chore or other and I ran off and had a copy made. It was considerably more dignified to be able to open the lock and walk in rather than have to climb up to remote latches and jimmy locks. Of course, there was no altruism involved in our actions, only selfish interest. When we were not using the gym, we locked the door again so no other band of kids could come by and play. We wanted the place to ourselves.

Those keys to the Grant High School gym served me well for many years. When I was attending the University of Southern California, I would come home for Christmas and, like so many other college students, work at the post office. I pulled the graveyard shift, sorting mail at the railroad station, and usually we had most of the first batch finished by one or two o'clock. So a bunch of us would take off and go over to Grant. I would let us into the gym and we would turn on the lights and play for a couple of hours. After that, we would go back to the station, toss around some newly arrived mail sacks for a couple of hours and then go home to sleep.

Later, when I got my first coaching job at Benson High in Portland, I still had my key to the Grant gym. The rules limited us to a few hours of practice during the afternoon and that was not enough for me. I scheduled a few extra sessions in the mornings and evenings at my alma mater. Luckily, they didn't change the locks even once in all those years.

But finding a place to play was not all that consumed a lot of our energy in those days. Fighting to be allowed to play was just as important. In high school, for instance, there was a regulation that members of the school team could not play on any church league or scout troop teams in the city. As a result, most of the boys on the various high school teams played on their church teams without mentioning it, hoping their high school coaches would not find out. I may have overdone it a little.

There was, as I recall, a Baptist League, a Catholic Youth Organization League, a B'nai B'rith League, a Methodist League, a Presbyterian League and maybe one or two others. I played in them all. You had to have some affiliation with the church to be eligible so I had some very busy Sundays. I would start with an early mass at one of the Catholic churches in town, bicycle over to a Sunday School at Grant Park Baptist, then go to another one at Westminster Presbyterian, catch an afternoon sermon at Rose City Methodist and maybe wind up at a Sunday night young people's meeting at Calvin Lutheran. By the time the day was over, I was eligible for every church league in Portland. Luckily, the B'nai B'rith did not have to be worked in on Sunday.

Many players on almost all the teams were no more eligible by reason of their religion than I was. I remember one game that I played for Westminster Presbyterian when we really loaded up with outsiders. Our opponents on another church team were furious because we had six ringers and they had only four.

To make sure we wouldn't be found out and made ineligible by the public school authorities, we all used false names when we played in the various church leagues. We needed different names for our different teams and the danger was forgetting which name you were using for which church. I tried to keep some link between my aliases by always using O-something: O'Hara, O'Brien, O'Hallihan and so on. I became known to my friends as the Great O.

This has been a part of my life, it seems, from that day until this and I have never been able to accept it or get used to it. I simply do not understand, or have any tolerance for, people who put up barriers to keep other people from playing, whether it is the school board of Portland, Oregon, or the Amateur Athletic Union of the United States.

The AAU, which operates out of New York, was founded in 1888 at a time when there was no fine line between professional and amateur sports. It drew up regulations regarding amateur competition—and imposed penalties or even outright bans on athletes who broke them—and gained control of dozens of amateur sports in the United States. Such sports as boxing, bobsledding, gymnastics, horseshoe pitching, water polo, wrestling and even tug-of-war either are or have been under its jurisdiction, and the AAU was the American representative to the international organizations that controlled these sports—and to the Olympic Games.

In 1959, the Swedish federation had a great interest in American basketball and asked me, as the coach of its national team and as an American, to arrange a tour of the United States. This was something I thought would benefit everybody: the Swedes would play some top American collegiate competition, the United States would get a rare chance to see a foreign team and I would get a trip home. I set up a ten-game schedule against American colleges.

The Swedish federation wrote the AAU asking permission and heard nothing. Not yes. Not no. Not no comment. Nothing. Ah, but after the team arrived in the United States, it heard plenty. The AAU thundered into action, objecting that these games had not been sanctioned and threatening all sorts of penalties against any college that played the Swedish team. The schools were particularly concerned with the possibility of their players being declared professionals, so they backed off. The tour had to be abandoned and the Swedish team returned home at a considerable financial loss.

That was the way the AAU operated, taking action that was arbitrary and destructive and against the interests of international sports competition whenever it felt its own power or authority threatened. This was particularly true when it came to Americans playing games in other countries. Take the matter of licenses. Now, I knew you needed a license to be a doctor or a lawyer or to drive a car, but I had known thousands of basketball players over the years and I had never heard of one who had a license. But if you wanted to compete outside the United States, said the AAU, you needed a license. Which it would be happy to provide for a nominal fee.

Then there was the question of travel permits. For some reason, you could play in Mexico or Canada without one, but if you wanted to arrange a game in any other country you needed a travel permit. Sold by the AAU. Very often, however, when you went to apply for one you were told that such permits were only issued when the AAU originated the competition. Which was like being told you needed a union card to get a job, but you had to have a job to get a union card. Or, as Yossarian said, "That's some catch, that Catch-22."

What was truly incomprehensible to me, though, was that the AAU's rules were far more restrictive than any other country's. Its practices varied widely from accepted international standards. If a club team anywhere in the world wanted to play a team from any other country, they just got together and played. No license, no travel permit, no official sanction necessary. Only when national teams met was there any protocol involved and even then it was arranged quickly. Abroad, the idea was that one of the purposes of a basketball federation was to stimulate and promote competition; the more that teams played each other, the better it was for everybody.

The tragedy was that the AAU's actions to limit competition between U.S. and foreign teams were almost totally effective. It is a sad fact that, from the time basketball was first designated an Olympic sport in 1936, it was more than thirty years before there was any regular exchange of teams between the United States and the rest of the world.

The United States has never bid to host the world's championship and has never been the site of a major international basketball tournament. I once took an Italian team to Sophia to a tournament that was being held in conjunction with an international sports festival. There were two things about it that stood out. In one week in Bulgaria, there was more international sports activity than had occurred in the United States since the 1932 Olympics took place in Los Angeles. And there was not a single American athlete competing in Bulgaria. There were delegations from places like China, Mongolia and Tibet, but none from the United States. Once every four years, we would get off our behinds and prepare for the Olympics—the AAU could hardly prevent that—but otherwise we just ignored the rest of the world.

When we did participate in international events, it was often with little planning or intelligence. For years, the AAU would choose as coach of the U.S. team in the world's championship a man whose main qualification was that he had lost the last time around. I guess they figured they were going to keep going with him until he got it right. Either that or they must have decided that all that experience as a loser made him the man for the job. This went on for three or four championships, in which the United States did not win a medal.

The battle to strip the AAU of its power was never really understood by the American public. It was generally portrayed as a simple power struggle between the AAU and the National Collegiate Athletic Association. That was certainly a part of it—especially when it came to which body was going to control our Olympic participation—but it was actually much more complex. It was all bound up in the organization of international sports.

In most countries, as I explained earlier, there is one organization for each major amateur sport: a basketball federation, a track and field federation, a soccer federation and so on. In the United States, alone of all the major countries, there was one organization in charge of everything: the AAU. If the AAU had been efficient and concerned about the sports for which it was responsible rather than only about its own power, this might not have been so bad. But, as it worked out, the whole of American participation in international athletics came down to one big jumbled pile on the desk of Dan Ferris, the long-time AAU boss.

And nobody really cared. Other nations often have several aggressive national newspapers and magazines devoted exclusively to sports news, but we have no real sports press as such. The most influential sportswriters are the syndicated ones in New York, where the AAU has its headquarters. The AAU organized a few track meets there and Ferris had a personal relationship of many years' standing with most of the top writers. Out in the hinterlands, of course, all people really cared about was how Illinois was going to do against Indiana, and the like. Except for the Olympics, there was no tradition of international competition to raise excitement.

After the Swedish tour was cancelled, I told officials there to make a formal application to the international basketball federation for suspension of the AAU on the grounds of abuse of authority. I filed a personal slander suit of my own against Ferris and his friends, who had called me a sports promoter in disrepute, which I did not think was very friendly of them. I doubt that these actions bothered the AAU particularly. It could hardly have felt threatened by a small federation and a lone coach.

But, the truth is, the AAU had at long last made a serious miscalculation. A weak and ineffective organization in the most powerful sports country on earth had long been a disaster internationally and our battle against it soon received the help of the one man in the world capable of winning: R. W. Jones.

Jones possessed two traits that were extremely important in the fight against the AAU. One was his single-mindedness in doing exactly what he thought was necessary to the advancement of basketball. The other was his genius at compromise in order to achieve those ends. I have seen him enter world basketball congresses and international meetings where the most explosive issues were being discussed and work out peaceful solutions in the best interests of the game. Every time a conflict threatened to splinter the international federation, R. W. Jones would resolve it.

For more than twenty years, for instance, the Latin American countries felt that Europe was dominating the game in spite of the fact that Jones gave the Latin Americans more than their share of world championships. They demanded that international federation headquarters be moved to Latin America and considered breaking away altogether. Jones, by sheer force of personality, headed this off and kept the federation from breaking up.

The political conflicts that provoked so many problems in other sports were kept under control by Jones. He was absolutely consistent in his view that if any country refused to play a scheduled opponent for a political reason it would be fined or suspended. He was devious at times and he came up with more than one tricky solution, but he never failed. Jones was a wizard at parliamentary manipulation. He may not have written *Robert's Rules of Order*, but he knew how to get from them precisely what he wanted.

There was the time when the Philippines were awarded the world tournament in the late 1950s. The Philippine government made it known that Yugoslavia would not be welcome because Manila had no diplomatic relations with any of the communist countries. Jones told the Philippine federation that no member country could be denied participation in the tournament, but the federation could hardly tell its government what to do. Jones' compromise was to move the championships elsewhere, but to let the Philippines host an "invitational" tournament of its own. Yugoslavia was not invited.

Jones faced the Formosa question, the North and South Korea question, the East and West Germany question and handled them all. The communist countries said he favored the capitalists and the capitalist countries said he favored the communists. The truth is, he was so respected on both sides that he generally got whatever he wanted.

Jones' biggest headache in recent years concerned Israel and South Africa. Countries that sided with the Arabs did not want to play Israel. When the time came for the European championships, Jones seeded Israel into a group of nations friendly to it, thereby reducing the chances Israel would have to play any hostile nation before elimination from the tournament. But if such games did occur, Jones insisted they take place and they almost always did.

As for South Africa, Jones simply recognized that there was no way in the world the black African nations would play against that country. So he would take an occasional inspection trip and afterwards state that South Africa had not met international regulations for integrating its teams. Yet he resisted all efforts to kick South Africa out of the international federation.

By the late 1950s, Jones had become determined to curb the AAU; once he did, there was nothing that could keep it from happening, even if it did take nearly twenty years. Jones had wearied of dealing with an organization with so many irons in the fire. Dan Ferris did not answer his letters any faster than he did anyone else's and Jones wanted an organization that was concerned solely with basketball, as all the other countries had.

After three years, the Swedish motion against the AAU was finally placed on the agenda of the World Basketball Congress in Rome. The AAU did a considerable amount of lobbying to get it killed, but Jones was determined that the question be faced. At last, the AAU saw it was hopeless and, the day before the motion was to be voted on, turned over a check for $8,000 to the Swedish federation—which covered losses for the cancelled tour—and agreed to invite the Swedish national team to the United States, all expenses paid.

It was another four years before my suit against the AAU was finally decided. The judge agreed I had been slandered, but did not award me the damages I was seeking because I could not prove malice. I was, alas, ahead of my time. Just over a decade later, a coach in Oregon got involved in a dispute with the AAU over an exchange of wrestling teams with foreign countries. It ended up in the courts and he was awarded $130,000.

When I discussed the Swedish motion with Jones, I told him of my past experiences with the AAU and asked him why something wasn't done about its negative influence. I was surprised to hear him say, "Why don't you do something about it?"

"Me?" I said. "What can I do? They don't know me in the

U.S. I haven't even been home for years."

But Jones was awfully persuasive. The greatest potential for fighting the AAU, he said, was in the colleges. That was where the coaches, the players and the publicity were. Therefore, that was where the power was. Go to the national coaches' meeting, he said. Have them put the whole question of the AAU on the agenda. Get them to pass a resolution against it. And in 1959, I did go to the coaches' convention at the NCAA basketball tournament in San Francisco, where I lobbied for a motion that a U.S. basketball federation be formed to replace the AAU as America's representative in international competition. It passed overwhelmingly.

But for all his power and for all the support he had within U.S. basketball circles, Jones had to move slowly when it came to ousting the AAU. There were several large obstacles in his path. One was the nature of the bureaucracy he had helped to create. The international federation was composed of officials who were jealous and protective of their own authority. In every country, there were rival factions fighting for power. No group in control was going to be quick to recognize another member country's challenge for fear of establishing a precedent that might come back to haunt it.

Then there was the fact that Jones did not have unanimous support for his wish to see stronger U.S. participation in international basketball. That certainly was the last thing the Soviet Union wanted and it controlled a lot of votes.

But Jones never gave up. Every Olympic year, the international federation would hold its meeting and every time the question of which body should represent the United States would come up. Between meetings, Jones lobbied and persuaded and brought more member countries into line. The NCAA, in the meantime, became more and more interested in wresting away from the AAU control of all sports, and put more of its energy and muscle into the effort. Finally, in 1972 in Munich, it happened. The U.S. Basketball Association was recognized as America's official representative for the sport.

If I was expecting this to be the answer to all of my problems and to inaugurate the golden age of American participation in international basketball, I am afraid the reality has been a little less exciting. There are times, in fact, when I wonder what I spent my time fighting for. The AAU used to charge $2 for a permit to tour and $4 to license a player. The ABAUSA charges $200 a month to tour and from $50 to $1,500 for a license. Why either of these items should cost anything is something I still don't understand.

The truth is, I guess, that one bureaucracy is pretty much like another. There will always be those who play and coach and organize and those who administer and regulate and control. I suppose I will never lose the distrust I have always had of the few who put up barriers to keep the many from playing. It goes back to the days when I was locked out of all those gyms.

Anyway, things are somewhat better than when the AAU was in charge. At least, the ABAUSA answers its mail.

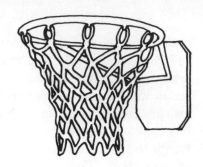

CHAPTER **11**

Me and the CIA

I AM NOT NOW, nor have I ever been, a member of the CIA. If I have, they owe me twenty-five years' back pay.

I feel I have to make this statement because, every so often, a left-wing paper in one country or another will intimate that my role as a basketball coach is really only a disguise for my true mission—to foment trouble. I must admit that the accusations do have a certain plausible ring. In all the years I have been travelling, I have had a remarkable affinity for being where the trouble was.

I was in Hungary, the Congo and Libya just before the revolutions. I was in Bolivia during two coups. (Actually, it was difficult in those days to be in Bolivia when there was not a coup.) I was in Kuwait during the Arab-Israeli six-day war and shortly after I left Morocco somebody tried to assassinate the king. I was in Poland during food strikes and in Paris during violent student demonstrations. I lived through one revolutionary change of government in Turkey and half a dozen in Peru.

Even when I was just passing through a country en route to another, I have had problems. On the way to Melbourne for the 1956 Olympics, I was among the people chased by a Singapore mob into the Raffles Hotel where a handful of British soldiers had to protect us. And when I got to Jakarta on that same trip,

I looked Dutch enough to be detained and stripped at the airport.

Having made my protestations, I must confess to the one contact with the CIA I did have over the years. It happened in Turkey where I had been invited, in 1959, to train the national team for the Rome Olympics the following year. I was also able to line up a club coaching job there and another as dean of students at Robert American College in Istanbul. Turkey had a nucleus of good players and the fact that they all lived in and around Istanbul made it easy to train together for a long period. I was hopeful of making a good showing in Rome.

I also became involved in basketball at the college where, in addition to the American students, there was a large group from other foreign countries. Iraq, in particular, was well represented by sons of officials of a government that had recently been voted out of power. Early in the fall, some of these Iraqi students came to me with the idea of forming a team and visiting Baghdad in the spring to play against some local clubs. It sounded fine to me —I had never been to Baghdad—so I helped them arrange the trip and we got together a few times a week during the fall and winter to practice.

Sometime in February, six or seven weeks before we were supposed to leave, the Iraqis began coming in, one by one, to cancel out. One student said it was too hot in Baghdad at that time of year. Another said it was the rainy season. Somebody else had examinations. Everybody had some excuse. When I tried to put it all together, all I could conclude was that each student was the son of a person of influence and each had a different reason for not wanting to go home. Somebody, I thought, ought to know this.

In Istanbul, it was easy to identify the current CIA man. He was always hanging around the pool at the Hilton, which overlooked the harbor, keeping an eye on Russian shipping through binoculars. And he always spoke with a Harvard accent. I swam often at the Hilton pool so I knew exactly who my man was. I went to the hotel and looked him up.

"Excuse me, Mr. CIA man," I said. "I've got something that I think might interest you."

He pretended he didn't know what I was talking about and kept staring out to sea through his binoculars. But he listened and I told my story.

"Look, professor," he said when I had finished, "why don't you take care of the university and we'll take care of things in our jurisdiction."

I shrugged and walked away.

Weeks later, just about at the time we were supposed to have played basketball in Baghdad, there was an anti-Western coup in Iraq. Questions were raised on the floor of Congress, demanding to know why the United States had not been aware of it. My conscience was certainly clear.

Alas, that was not the only coup that occurred while I was in Turkey. About six weeks before we were to go to the Olympics, the country went to bed with one government in power and woke up with another. For days, the radio broadcast martial music and patriotic announcements. What affected me the most was a decree forbidding the gathering of more than three people in any one place at the same time. For a while, I was actually coaching an Olympic basketball team two at a time. Two players would show up and we would work out for a while. Then they would leave and two more would practice. It was far from ideal, but you should have seen our one-on-one.

In the end, the new government decided that, as a measure of economy and sacrifice, it would send to the Olympics only those competitors who stood a reasonable chance of winning a medal. Prior to that, Turkey had sent a small army of athletes, but I have an idea the government was concerned that, given the political situation, fewer might return home from Rome than went. At any rate, our basketball team was good, but not that good and I ended my association with the Turkish basketball federation in Rome without my team, as its official observer only.

For the second time, I had come close to coaching in the Olympics, only to miss out at the last minute. It would not be the last time.

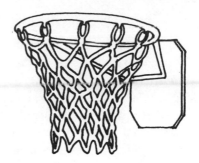

CHAPTER **12**

Peru's Who

EARLY IN 1960, I returned to the United States and did some lecturing arranged by the University of Wisconsin, where I became friendly with Bud Foster, its basketball coach. One of his former players was working in Peru and had become involved with the sport there. The basketball federation asked him if he knew of any American coaches who spoke Spanish; when he relayed the request to Foster, I was recommended. It was a quirk of fate that led to four of the most enjoyable years of my life.

Unlike Italy, Peru is a country that is totally dominated by one city so I rarely had to travel outside Lima. As practice sessions were held at night, I had a great deal of free time. I played thirty-six holes of golf a day and got in a lot of swimming as well. And, because the cost of living was so low, I was able to live very handsomely. I had a lovely apartment in the Lima suburb of Mira Flores—literally, "Look at the flowers"—where the country's wealthiest people lived in homes as luxurious as the best that Beverly Hills had to offer.

An entire family came with the apartment. The people I rented it from insisted that they be kept on or they would have no place to go. The man did the gardening and took care of the car, his wife did the cooking and their daughter helped out with the

81

housework. I studied French at the Alliance Française and advanced Spanish at the Catholic University of Peru and soon discovered that, in Latin America, the traditional afternoon siesta is very often spent in bed, but not always sleeping. No antebellum southern plantation owner ever lived any better.

When I arrived, the state of basketball in Peru was quite low, but I had two elements in my favor from the start. One was the support of an ambitious young federation president, Guillermo Toro Lira, who was determined to build the sport and with whom I quickly became friendly. The other was the greatest legacy any coach has ever been handed: five basketball-playing brothers, all at or coming into their primes. They were the Duartes, sons of Italian immigrants who ranged in height from six feet three to six feet nine, and in ability from good to excellent. The best was Ricardo Duarte, who went on to become the leading scorer in the 1964 Olympics.

One of the Duarte brothers, Enrico, had been on the Peruvian national team before I became the coach, but the rest of the players were older and slower. I could see that I would have to do the same thing I had done in Italy: build a completely new team according to my own specifications. The players would have to be young, fast, willing to learn and possess tremendous desire to win. With the five brothers as a nucleus, I put together a team that had only two holdovers: Enrico Duarte and Simon Paredis. Paredis was a conscientious player with some skill, but I felt he was not quick enough for my pressing, gambling, fast-breaking game. However, he played for a club that had considerable political influence in Peruvian basketball circles, so there was quite a bit of pressure to include him and finally I did. It was a decision I would come to regret.

The team got off to a tremendous start. The players took to my aggressive, pressing style of play immediately and began a competitive climb that would soon place them among the top teams in Latin America. We defeated Mexico, Panama and Canada for the first time in the country's history and tied for first in the South American championships, Peru's best all-time showing. We also placed a creditable fourth in the Pan-American Games and did well in the world championships in Brazil against an American team that included future NBA players Willis Reed, Don Kojis and Gary Bradds, losing by only five or six points. We made two extended tours of the United States during which we played some of the top college teams in the country. Though we did not beat any of the major powers, we certainly had nothing to be ashamed of. Considering where the team had been when we started, it was a very heady couple of years for all of us.

And interesting.

We went to a tournament in Paraguay where I had a lesson they don't teach in coaching clinics: the danger of neglecting your halftime defense. We had a six-point lead against the host team going into the locker room at the intermission, but emerged to find we were trailing by one. I could have run over and screamed at the scorekeeper and gotten shrugs in return. Or I could have screamed at the scoreboard itself and not even have received that satisfaction. What I did instead was take one of the players off the bench and tell him to sit by the scoreboard so nothing else could happen.

We took the lead again and, just as we were going down the court on a fast break, the lights went out. We lost the basket we were about to score, we lost the ball and, by the time the lights went on, we had lost five points again. My guy watching the scoreboard had been helpless in the dark.

I pulled another player off the bench and told him to sit by the light switch. I would not be able to keep losing players like this much longer, but they were more valuable watching the scoreboard and the lights than they would have been on the court.

Once again, we took a three-point lead and once again we had the ball when, with about two minutes left, the entire bleachers on one side of the floor collapsed. Players on both teams rushed over to help and began pulling people out of the wreckage. Finally, order was restored and we all were relieved to see that no one was hurt. Then I looked at the scoreboard again. Instead of two minutes left, there were ten seconds. Instead of leading by three points, we were trailing by two. I hardly had to guess to whom the referees were going to give the ball. Graciously, I accepted defeat.

But by far the most remarkable game my Peruvian team ever played was in the Bolivar Games—an important regional tournament for many of the countries in the northern part of Latin America—in Barranquilla, Colombia. The court was an armed camp because in a game played there shortly before the tournament, a referee had been attacked by the crowd and one of his eyes had been gouged out. The Colombian authorities had surrounded the court with soldiers carrying rifles, which cast a decidedly unsportsmanlike tone over the whole affair.

We played Colombia in an early game and raced off to a big lead, which kept the fans reasonably subdued. But, late in the first half, Colombia put in one of its youngest players, who was not only tall and strong but quite talented as well. The tide began to turn. As the gap on the scoreboard got smaller and smaller, the crowd got wilder and wilder. The soldiers ringing the court turned out to be fans first and guardians of the peace second as they shouted and gestured their team on. There are two kinds of gestures in situations like this—the kind made without rifles and the kind made with them. Since the soldiers were making the latter, those of us who were not Colombians were extremely intimidated.

What surprised me most about the entire situation, however, was the impartiality of the referees. I had never seen a game called more fairly under such trying circumstances. Even the fact that the Colombian team was screaming at every call against it, thereby inflaming the crowd even more, did not seem to intimidate the referees. Since the fate of their recent predecessors in the arena had to be on their minds, I could only conclude that this referee from Panama and his colleague from Puerto Rico had to be two of the bravest men in the world.

At the end of the half, we still had a six-point lead and retired to our locker room. Later, both teams were back on the court taking their warm-up shots when the buzzer went off, signalling the start of the second half. The players walked to mid-court for the tipoff only to find something missing: the referees. The officials went to their dressing room and knocked on the door. No answer. They opened the door. Nobody inside.

They did find, however, an open window. The referees had climbed out the window, hailed a taxi and headed for the airport and the first plane out of Colombia. The game had to be abandoned. The official records of the Bolivar Games take note of the time Peru beat Colombia by the low score of 38–32. Given that edge, we went on to win the tournament—after officials had rounded up some more referees.

Colombia had no monopoly on Latin America's excitable fans. The Peruvians themselves were far from docile. In fact, the worst riot I ever saw took place while I was in Peru. And it had nothing to do with basketball. I was in our office at the Lima stadium during a hotly contested soccer game when the fans took exception to a referee's decision and began throwing things out onto the field. To look at the security arrangements at most of the big Latin American soccer stadiums, you would think it almost impossible for any real trouble to break out. Many Latin American stadiums have moats surrounding the playing field. In Lima, there was a high fence. But you must never underestimate the ingenuity of the Latin American fan. There are always several willing to climb the highest fence or swim the deepest moat to pay their respects to the referee.

This time, though, the situation was made worse by a freak accident of timing. The gates, kept closed during the game to keep out non-ticket holders, were thrown open with about five minutes left to make it easier for people to leave. Unfortunately, this also allowed the many kids hanging around outside the stadium to run in to see the last few minutes of action. And in this game, the riot broke out inside at the same time the gates were opened outside.

The police began throwing tear gas to disperse the crowd, which began rushing toward the exits just as a mob of kids, excited by the noise and impatient to see what was going on, was racing up the ramps. The two masses of people collided in the midst of all the tear gas. The end result was 400 people trampled to death and hundreds more wounded.

As will happen anywhere that this kind of trouble involving tens of thousands of people erupts, riots and looting broke out. The next thing I knew our office in the stadium was being invaded. I was not about to risk my life for a typewriter so I managed to work my way outside the stadium just in time to see part of the mob attack the Goodyear plant headquarters across the street. It was the handiest symbol of American imperialism, I guess, and pretty soon there were shouts of, "Get the gringo! Burn it down!"

The coolest head in the whole situation, I later learned, belonged to the general manager of the plant. He had no wish to be a hero either. So he just took off his coat, mussed up his hair, rubbed some dirt on his shirt and stood against the wall behind the door in his office. When the mob burst through, he slid into the crowd, fired a pistol into the air, and shouted, "Get the gringo!" Then he slipped away in the confusion. If he hadn't thought so quickly, he would have been a dead man.

Similar situations involving U.S. citizens in Latin America occurred from time to time while I was there, especially when the political climate got hot. Once, I was making a tour of Venezuela when some rebel groups were making coordinated attacks on U.S. properties. Shortly after I had given a clinic at a high school, I was later told, one of these groups arrived with the idea of kidnapping me. My visit to the country had received quite a lot of press attention and I suppose they figured I would make a highly visible captive. But their timing was off, so they charged over to a nearby Sears outlet and kidnapped the store manager instead. After a long round of negotiations, which were publicized all over the world, Sears finally paid a ransom and the manager was released.

Now, if you are the manager of a Sears store, publicity like this is of absolutely no value to you. All your superiors care about is the health of your sales. But I thrive on publicity and I have often wondered how much mileage I could have gotten out of the incident had the rebels kidnapped me as intended. On the other hand, who would have paid to ransom me? Not the Peruvian basketball federation. Maybe it was just as well.

As part of my duties in Peru, I once gave a clinic in an Amazon rain forest. Basketball among the Indians there was about as primitive as the countryside. The players were enthusiastic, but so isolated that they seldom received any real training or faced any decent competition. Also, the fact that the Indians loved to chew cocaine made it somewhat difficult to hold their attention long enough to teach them much.

There was one tournament scheduled for Iquitos, at the headwaters of the Amazon, which became the only one I know of ever to be called on account of rain. In that region, rain is like a lake being turned upside down; it hits with a force that literally knocks you over. It was too wet to get to the gym for basketball—and too wet for water polo or even submarine maneuvers.

While waiting for the rain to subside, I spent some time at the hotel with an American who collected snakes for U.S. zoos. He kept me awake with stories about how, after heavy rains, he often found the snakes he was looking for right in the bathtub in his room. When he went on to describe the deadly spiders that were also washed up by the torrents, I asked him if he ever found any dangerous creatures on airplanes. He said no, and I took the first one out of there.

Throughout my first few years in Peru, as the national team met with continued success and compiled the best record in its history, I began to discover one of the problems of winning. It makes losing that much more difficult to accept. It was during this period that the single most heartbreaking loss of my career occurred. We had just finished fourth in the 1963 Pan-American Games in São Paulo, Brazil, and went on to the world championships the following week in Rio de Janeiro. In a final-round qualifying game, we met Puerto Rico, the winner to go into the eight-team championship round. No Peruvian team had ever been there before. Puerto Rico had a strong team that was coached by Lou Rossini of New York University, an old friend.

We played one of our best games ever and with two seconds to go, we had a three-point lead and possession of the ball. If I had been Red Auerbach, I would have been halfway through my victory cigar. Then Ricardo Duarte, who was being double-teamed, whirled to protect the ball and was called for charging. It was the first and last time in my life I ever saw that infraction called when the pivot man's foot was stationary. To make things worse, it put Ricardo out of the game. Still, even if Puerto Rico made both free throws we would win.

The first foul shot was good, but the second one missed and we got the rebound. I breathed a sigh of relief; the game was all but over. But then there was another whistle. The referee called one of our players for stepping into the foul lane too early, something that is very seldom called in international play. Puerto Rico was awarded another shot. This one missed, too, but our players, nervous about stepping in too soon again, stayed back a fraction of a second. A Puerto Rican player reached in for the rebound and made the basket that tied the game. Without Ricardo, we lost in overtime.

The defeat cast a pall over what had been a successful showing in two important tournaments, but our spirits were buoyed somewhat when we returned home to a heroes' welcome. Then, however, disaster struck again. Guillermo Toro Lira called me into his office.

"Great news," he said. "Our bid to host the women's world championships in Lima next year has been accepted."

"Wonderful," I said. "Congratulations."

"And because of the fine work you've done with the men's team, we want you to coach the women's team in the tournament."

"Wait a minute. I coached the team, but I'm not a miracle worker. All the women I've seen here are short, slow and can't shoot. Wait until you see the Russian women's team. You should get one of your saints for this job."

But I was elected. There have been a lot of disasters in Peru over the years: floods, earthquakes, landslides and the conquistadors. But none of them could have topped the country's participation in the women's world championships.

The average size of the Peruvian women was five feet four, and one look at them on the court told you that there were no Duarte sisters. They were light years behind the ability of the best women's teams and had no business out on the court with the top seven countries in the world. Only the fact that the host country's team automatically qualified for the tournament put them there. To make things worse, our first game was against the Russians.

It was the only time I ever saw any pity on the part of a Soviet sports team. They tried to be kind. They fumbled on offense, stepped out of the way on defense, even passed the ball to us from time to time. But it was hopeless. Their center was seven feet tall. Ours was five-five. The score was something like 80–20. It could easily have been 200–0.

In a sense, though, the tournament was a success. Attendance was high and the federation made enough money to construct a new basketball arena. Also, interest in women's basketball became quite intense in Peru after the tournament ended and today its teams are internationally respected. More so than the men's teams, in fact.

While I was involved in this disaster, I was still coaching the men's team and sowing the seeds of my own destruction. We played very well all through 1964, qualifying for the Olympics for the first time in the country's history. Once more, I had a chance to coach a team in the Olympics. I was looking forward eagerly to the trip to Tokyo.

One of our last games before leaving for Japan was a tune-up against Chile. Just before the game, Guillermo Toro Lira walked up to me on the court. He wanted Simon Paredis to see a lot of action in the game, he said. I was stunned. Not because whether or not Paredis played meant anything in an exhibition game, but because it was the first time Toro Lira had ever told me how to handle the team.

"Guillermo, that is direct interference with my authority," I said. "You sit up there and watch the game and I'll coach the team."

It was Jim McGregor at his diplomatic best. If I had been older and wiser, I would have agreed to play Paredis, put him in for a short time and forgotten the whole thing. Instead, I challenged Toro Lira. He gave me an angry look and returned to his seat.

The game began and we ran off to an early lead. Every once in a while, I would sneak a look up at Toro Lira in the stands and I could see that he was furious. He was surrounded by federation people and it seemed likely that he must have promised them that Paredis—who played for an influential club team, remember—would play. For that reason alone, I decided that Paredis would stay on the bench. During the second half, as our winning margin continued to mount, I was handed a note:

Put Simon Paredis in at once.
Guillermo Toro Lira

That did it. I stood up, turned around and caught Toro Lira's eye. I held the note up high. Then I tore it up and scattered the pieces. The game ended, and so did my career as coach of the Peruvian national team—in the midst of a shouting match on the floor of the arena.

The press was outraged and at first the coach Toro Lira picked to replace me said he would not accept the job. But Toro Lira was sure of his power and eventually my support dissolved. I was the foreigner, after all, who had challenged the authority of the local man who had done so much to lead Peru into international basketball respectability. For the third time I had come very close to being an Olympic coach and for the third time I had lost out.

In Tokyo, Peru won a big upset over Brazil and then proceeded to lose to teams it should have beaten. I stayed around for a few months to wind up my affairs and when I went in to get my final paycheck I ran into Toro Lira. The bitterness between us seemed forgotten and, after a few words, he reached into his pocket, pulled something out and handed it to me. It was a gold medal, made up in appreciation of my services to Peruvian basketball. He and I have been good friends ever since and he has sent several good players to my touring teams over the years. He is the number-one man for all sports in Peru today.

My four years in Peru taught me something about job security. Coaches sometimes think they have it rough, but I outlasted close to a dozen heads of state. In fact, I think Toro Lira got more heat for firing me than some generals ran into when they staged a coup in front of the presidential palace.

CHAPTER **13**

Lost in Las Cruces

AFTER MORE THAN A DECADE in Europe and Latin America, I began to wonder about the future. As much as I enjoyed travelling and living in foreign countries, I could see there was no security and there were moments when I had serious doubts about my ability to keep on finding the challenging and rewarding opportunities that had always seemed to come my way. The idea of having a real home, establishing some coaching roots and becoming a permanent part of a community somewhere seemed more and more appealing.

Early in 1965, I went to Portland to visit my mother. I got an earful of, "What kind of son are you? I never see you. Why do you want to stay thousands of miles away all the time?" Although I had come home for a short time only, those words hit me hard. I made up my mind to see what I could find in the United States.

The NCAA basketball championships were being held in Portland at that very time, which meant that nearly every major-college coach and athletic director in the country was in town. And if anybody had forgotten who I was, the morning paper interviewed me and ran a long story on its front sports page, headlined "McGregor Comes Home." When I wandered by the coaches' convention headquarters, everybody had seen it and I received friendly greetings all around.

It didn't take long to discover that the head coaching job at New Mexico State was open and I asked some of my basketball friends about it. After all that time abroad, I didn't really imagine I could be a serious contender for a major-college job, but nearly everybody I asked disagreed. Apply, I was told. You're sure to get the job. I couldn't understand why they were so confident. Surely, there would be hundreds of coaches applying for a job like this one. But I looked up Warren Woodson, the New Mexico State athletic director. His first question took me by surprise.

"Are you a Christian?" he wanted to know.

"Yes," I said, wondering what he could make of that sort of qualification.

"Are you Baptist?" he asked.

"My mother is," I said.

"I want to meet her."

I have applied for a lot of jobs in my career, but that is the only time anyone ever wanted to meet my mother. I took him out to her home and was happy to see that they got along famously. They were both Texans and both Southern Baptists. After a brief conversation, during which they said whatever it is that Southern Baptists say to each other, Woodson turned and gave me a long penetrating look.

"You're my man," he said.

I was elated, of course, but still surprised I had gotten the job so easily after having been overseas for so long. When I told this to a coaching friend, his reply—that my being away had probably helped me get the job—puzzled me a little. So did the fact that I couldn't find anyone else who seemed to have been a candidate. I began to hear a few other disturbing things. That the coach I was replacing, Presley Askew, was widely respected, but had had clashes with Woodson. That the basketball facilities at New Mexico State were not very good and that basically it was a football school. And that the football coach was none other than Warren Woodson.

I also began to wonder why no visits to the campus had been arranged and why I hadn't met with a selection committee or the president of the school—all normally part of the hiring process. But none of these things occurred to me until after I had gotten the job. By then I was too pleased about being home again to worry much about anything besides recruiting players and developing a schedule.

The feeling of euphoria ended the moment I got to Las Cruces. I don't think I will ever forget my reception there. A hitchhiker through town could not have been more ignored. There wasn't a word in the papers or any sort of get-together arranged with school officials or the media. The nearest I got to an official welcome was the remark of the desk clerk at my motel. When he found out who I was, he said, "They should have hired Lou Henson."

This was something I was to hear about twice a day during my entire stay at New Mexico State. Lou Henson had won several state high school basketball championships at Las Cruces and had gone on to a successful tenure at Abilene Christian. Everyone I met seemed disappointed that he hadn't gotten the job and I was quickly known as Warren Woodson's boy. It was not a label I aspired to willingly; our relationship deteriorated from the very first day.

I went over to the campus and met Woodson in the new football offices that had just been built near the stadium. They were large, pleasant and air-conditioned. We exchanged a few words and then he offered to show me my office, which was in the stadium itself. It turned out to be a tiny closet hidden under a far corner of the bleachers, between the laundry room and the boiler. New Mexico is only a few degrees cooler than hell most of the time and I doubt if there is anyone in the state who would submit willingly to being placed between two artificial sources of heat. It was the worst office I had ever seen and the most ridiculous place imaginable to try to convince a prospective player of the joys awaiting him playing basketball at New Mexico State.

I mentioned this to Woodson as diplomatically as I could, but he quickly ended that part of the conversation by saying, "I thought you'd be different, more appreciative."

After that, I don't think there was a single item—large or small —that Woodson and I didn't fight over.

Large thing: I wanted an assistant coach. Fine, he said, but all we can pay is $150 a month. Who on earth would work for $150 a month? I protested. He didn't know, but that was all he would pay. I did, in fact, find a graduate assistant willing to work for those wages, but it didn't take him long to size up the situation. Whatever time he didn't spend helping me coach, he spent recruiting players—for the football team.

Small thing: I wanted business cards, something to prove to a prospect and to his parents who I was. Just a little nicety. Unnecessary expense, said Woodson.

Large thing: I wanted to develop a strong schedule, since that is a good way to attract quality players. Fine, said Woodson, schedule anyone you want. But we can only pay a $350 guarantee at home because the gym only seats 1,500 people. But you can play anywhere in the United States you want, as long as you can pay for the trip. So I put together a schedule that had us opening on the road against Bradley, Wichita and Kansas—a sure way to start out with three losses—and later bolstering the home records of Utah, Brigham Young, Wyoming, Texas Western, New Mexico and many others. Our arch rival was Texas Western, which won the NCAA title that year. Our number-two rival was New Mexico, which went to the National Invitational Tournament. No sooner had I put together the schedule than Basketball News rated it the toughest in the country.

Small thing: I wanted to organize a booster club. I had never seen a college where there was less interest in basketball. Booster clubs were for football, said Woodson. Stay in your boiler room.

Recruiting was another problem. The players back from the previous year were quite poor—the team had only won a couple of games—and in those days you couldn't use freshmen on varsity rosters. This meant I had to build for the following years, and try to find enough junior-college transfers who would be immediately eligible, in order to salvage what I could out of the season coming up.

Luckily, New Mexico was so sparsely populated that anybody could be admitted to the school who had a high school degree and showed "signs of maturity." And, in fact, I was able to put together a pretty fair freshman team. It could certainly beat the varsity easily enough. But I had been away too long to have enough good junior-college contacts and it was difficult to lure any first-rate prospects who could help immediately.

The details of the season are too painful to report in any detail, but the bottom line was a record of 4–21. Making things even worse was the fact that my war with Woodson never abated. If anything, it got more heated as the season wore on. He dealt in threats and complaints and continuous demonstrations of how tough he was. You would do things his way—and without argument—or you would be gone. I, of course, was not exactly the stolid, uncomplaining, long-suffering Baptist he thought he was getting.

At one point, I met my predecessor, Presley Askew, who was getting on in years and was still at the school in an administrative job in the admissions department. I mentioned the trouble I was having with Woodson and he began to tremble.

"I'm a Christian," this kind, respected coach said. "I'm a good man. This is the only person in my life I hate. I hate this man."

Finally, the boiler room and the bad feelings and the losses took their toll. There was a two-week break for exams before the final two games of the season and I went in to see Woodson. I told him a new opportunity had come up and, if it was all the same to him, I would like to leave before those last two games were played. That was fine with him, he said, and he added something to the effect that I would not be missed. Only later did I learn that he had pretended not to know that I had left and had made it look as if I had run out on the team, rather than having received his permission.

Then New Mexico State did what it should have done in the first place. It hired Lou Henson as both basketball coach and athletic director. Within a couple of years, he built both a fine new fieldhouse and an excellent basketball program. Warren Woodson was back in Texas.

And I was out on the street again. My remarks to Woodson that a new opportunity was waiting for me had been just so much bravado. But, unbeknownst to me, it turned out to be the truth. I was soon involved in my life's work.

PART TWO

The Merchant of Happiness

Gulf, St. Peter and
We Shall Overcome

I REACTED TO THE LOSS of my second American college coaching job the same way I had to my first one: I wrote a lot of letters. Only instead of writing to fifty international airlines as I had after being fired at Whitworth, this time I wrote to fifty U.S. companies which did a lot of business abroad. The letter was brief. It described how basketball was developing all over the world, how press and television coverage was growing and how fans were beginning to flock to arenas everywhere. A company that sponsored an American touring team to play foreign club teams, I said, would reap a lot of favorable publicity in foreign countries at a relatively modest cost.

This was not an idea that just popped into my head while I was sitting under an apple tree. The first man to take touring American teams abroad was Frank Walsh, at one time director of the Cow Palace in San Francisco where he organized some international tournaments. Frank was a man of tremendous energy and imagination with many sports contacts around the world. He took a couple of American all-star teams to South America in the late 1940s, and got into a lot of hot water with the AAU.

He envisioned travelling in Eastern Europe and elsewhere, but, given the political climate of the times and the fact that he could not drum up any major financial support, he was never able to organize his plan on a regular basis. But Frank Walsh was the real pioneer in this business.

Several companies replied to my letter, asking for more details, but I had little difficulty deciding which one interested me the most: Gulf Oil. It was known all over the world, was just beginning an aggressive marketing program in many countries and didn't seem likely to go out of business any time soon.

In my first encounter with Gulf, I had a crash course in going first class. I flew to the corporate headquarters in Pittsburgh, was met by a limousine and then whisked to a suite of hotel rooms permanently maintained for Gulf visitors. Soon, I was meeting with the vice president in charge of marketing and the vice president in charge of advertising and public relations.

The marketing vice president, a dynamic guy named Hoffman who wore a patch over one eye, was clearly the man in charge. "We've got to do something to humanize the concept of the seven sisters of the giant oil companies," he said. "The idea of having a basketball team that can get people cheering for Gulf sounds very promising. Tell me more about it."

I had a whole presentation planned, but after hearing that opening, I knew I was in. I gave Hoffman some of the details I had worked out for attracting players and setting up games and emphasized my international basketball contacts. After a few minutes of this, Hoffman said, "It sounds like a fine idea. Paul, I want to go ahead with this."

It was only then that I began to pay any real attention to the advertising director, who had been quietly listening to Hoffman and me. He was Paul Sheldon and he was the man I worked with during the four years of my Gulf sponsorship. I don't think I've ever met anyone more friendly or helpful. During our entire association, he was always there to pull me out of trouble.

Paul and I conferred for the next couple of days, setting up the details and deciding how things would be handled. His biggest concern was that the tour be a class operation and that the players reflect favorably on the company. I was very excited when it was time to leave and start rounding up players; I must have been beaming when I went into Paul's office to say good-bye.

"Jim," he said, "I want you to know that I'm all for Gulf sponsoring this team, in spite of the fact that I saw your New Mexico State team play once."

I looked at him for a moment and then we both burst out laughing.

"Well, I wish I hadn't," I said. And I was off.

In the early days of the tour, finding players was easy. The American Basketball Association had not been born yet and the NBA had only nine teams. It chose a maximum of twelve or fourteen players a year and I had my pick of much of the rest of the nation's 2,500 graduating seniors. When the ABA was formed, the quality of players I was able to take to Europe declined drastically. It was as if a huge vacuum appeared and sucked a lot of players off the market. It was not just the normal year-to-year stocking of two leagues with new draftees; suddenly, there were jobs for 120 new players. At the same time, the Vietnam war began getting serious and the draft robbed me of players, too. Fortunately for me, the caliber of basketball in Europe was not as high as it is today and the reserve of good college players was so large that my touring teams were still able to do well despite the talent gap created by the ABA.

The players on my touring teams seem to have turned a full 360 degrees since I first began taking them abroad in 1966. In the beginning, I got mostly clean-cut, well-mannered, educated young men, planning in the fall to try out for the NBA, to start graduate school or to enter some profession after a summer of playing basketball in Europe. They all looked about the same, dressed about the same and saw going to Europe as an educational experience. But gradually things began to change and at first I didn't know what to make of it.

In 1968, I was holding tryouts in New York when a young man walked up to me, stuck out his hand and said, "I'm Ken Grant from St. Peter's."

I took one look and said, "Son, you look like St. Peter himself." His hair seemed to flow down to his waist, he had a long beard and he was wearing beads. His companion, Mike Rowland, wore his hair in braids. They both looked Godawful to me.

"Who are you guys?" I said.

"We're basketball players," they said.

And damned if they weren't. Grant, in particular, moved well on the court, had a good quick pass and seemed very intelligent. But even if I had been ready for him on my team—and I wasn't— I knew Gulf Oil wouldn't be. I cut them both.

The following year, I had another tryout in New York and they showed up again. Once more, I was impressed with both of them, but I still couldn't handle their appearance. After the workout, I took them outside.

"Look," I said, "this is my bread and butter. I know you want to play and I like the way you play, but why do you look like that?"

"We're teachers," Grant said, "and it helps us relate to kids if we dress like this."

"But can't you shape up just a little?" I asked. "Just so people don't vomit every time you come out on the floor."

A couple of days later, they were back. They had cut their hair to about shoulder-length, trimmed their beards a little and put on clean faded jeans. I sighed and told them when to be ready to leave for Europe.

That was the beginning of my hippie basketball teams and of the further education of Jim McGregor. All my life, I came to realize, I had judged people by the way they talked and the way they looked—a stupid mistake. These kids turned out to be among the finest who ever played for me, completely unmaterialistic and wanting nothing more than to travel and live a carefree life. They played hard, they didn't complain about our crazy travelling schedule or an occasional missed meal and they didn't mind receiving only a small per diem and expenses. All they cared about was playing basketball and seeing the world.

I guess their philosophy was best expressed by Steve Rippe, who had played at the University of California at Santa Barbara. I asked him what he planned to do when the tour was over and he said, "Well, coach, I want to start at the bottom somewhere and work down."

Within a couple of years, the team consisted mainly of kids with long hair and beards, wearing jeans and carrying beat-up duffle bags containing banjos and guitars. Luckily for them and for me, I had acquired a perfect new sponsor by then: Levi's European division. All they asked was that the players wear Levi's at every opportunity to attract the young people of the countries we visited. As part of the deal, we could stock up on all the jeans and jackets we wanted at Levi's headquarters in Brussels. It was not long before my own resistance wore down and I began travelling around Europe in the latest denim outfits.

I will never forget some of those kids. There was Eddie Mast, a six-foot-nine center from Temple, who had been a number-three draft choice of the New York Knicks in 1969 and was the first white man I ever saw with an Afro. Eddie spent his entire bonus—several thousand dollars—on a motorcycle and showed up for the plane to Europe with two guitars and no shoes.

What astonished me the most was the way the girls flocked to these guys. We had never lacked for female attention on the tour before, but it had never been like this. The hippie girls seemed to appear out of nowhere and attach themselves to us, hitching rides and mooching meals. We were like a gypsy caravan, marching across Europe. The way they kept switching partners drove me nuts. In the first years of the tour, a girl would come along with a guy for a while and then disappear because they had broken up. But now I would see Mary with Joe a couple of times and then one day I would ask him, "How's Mary?"

"Oh, she's with Jack," he would say. "I'm with Joy now." They passed the girls around like cookies.

We had some problems during this era that didn't exist at other times. Some foreign team owners were alienated by our players' appearance and wouldn't schedule us; others gave me some heat about it. But as soon as the owners found that the

crowds weren't affected by the way the Levi's All-Stars looked—
that, in fact, curiosity seekers who didn't often go to basketball
games were showing up—we regained the ground we had lost and
stopped hearing complaints about the way we looked.

We never really solved our problem with hotels though. We
were never the perfect guests, what with a bunch of 200-pounders
tromping up and down the stairs and making noise late at night.
And when you added the impromptu guitar concerts, the tape-
recorded rock music and the gaggle of adoring females, the situation got worse. I would say we lost more hotels than ball games
during that era.

Things have come full circle since that time. The players of
today are much more like those of ten to twelve years ago, concerned about their careers or graduate school or their chances of
making the pros. Even Steve Rippe, the guy who wanted to start at
the bottom and work down, is the manager of a bank in San
Diego.

My last tie to that era was Ken Grant, who for seven or eight
years was my most trusted player. Whenever I had to split the
team or leave on other business, I put him in charge and he ran
the tour in my absence—even though my attempts to get him to
modify his haircut never really succeeded.

One interesting aspect of my years of touring is that I had a
minimum of racial problems. Even though it was a period when
black players seemed to be influenced by racial militancy back
home, this seldom caused any tension on the tour. On the rare
occasions when it did, I handled it as I would have any other
problem. It was the only thing I knew how to do.

During a practice session, one of the black players was dogging
it and I shouted at him the way I would have at anyone else:
"Come on, run! Get moving! Let's go! Full speed!"

The player stopped in the middle of the court and said very
dramatically, "Nobody's going to talk to me like that!"

I was astonished because it was the first time any player—black
or white—had challenged my authority as a coach. Undoubtedly,

someone with greater sensitivity to the situation or with training in psychology could have put it all back together, but I could not.

"You're right," I said. "Nobody's going to talk to you like that. You've got your ticket. Use it and go home."

And he did.

But even with a couple of incidents like that, in later years on the tour I found myself becoming closer to the black players than the white ones. The blacks had come up through the playgrounds the way I had, whereas many of the white players had upper-class backgrounds. Listening to the blacks made me realize that, if anything, I had closer ties to them than I did to many of the whites.

During the period of civil-rights turmoil, I sometimes kidded the black players when I saw them reading *The Autobiography of Malcolm X*, *The Fire Next Time* and *Burn, Baby, Burn*.

"Since I'm the handiest reminder of the white power structure around here," I would say, "I hope you guys aren't getting any ideas."

The truth is, the tour survived that era a lot better than did Watts or downtown Detroit. After a time, travelling together broke down whatever barriers there might have been, which is not to say there were no incidents.

We were eating lunch in a little town in Yugoslavia and, as it happened, the white players were sitting at one table and the blacks at another. None of us were aware of it, until a wild-eyed, thirtyish woman came up and started pounding on my head.

"You should be ashamed of yourself!" she screamed. "Introducing segregation here in Yugoslavia! This is a free state! A people's republic! You're disgracing America abroad!"

And all the time she kept banging me over the head. It turned out that she was a schoolteacher from somewhere in New England and I could never calm her down. The players, in the meantime, were doubled up with laughter.

"Boss, can we really sit with the white players?" the blacks said in broad plantation accents.

The whites began breaking out into alternate choruses of "Dixie" and "We Shall Overcome." I was waiting for the white ones to turn the tablecloths into Klan sheets and the black ones to start singing minstrel songs.

Finally, the woman got tired of hitting me. She moved to the center of the dining room where, I swear to God, there was a soapbox waiting, and she proceeded to give an oration that matched anything I've ever heard at Hyde Park.

CHAPTER 15

The King of Furbo

EARLY IN MY FIRST TOUR for Gulf, we went to Varese to play a club team owned by Giovanni Borghi, an important Italian industrialist. Starting from scratch after the war, he had built up an important home-appliances factory, the equivalent of General Electric in this country. But if refrigerators were Borghi's business, basketball was his passion. Nothing gave him greater pride than having developed his team, Ignis Varese, into the national club champion of Italy.

Borghi was somewhat embarrassed when we beat his team fairly handily, which may have convinced him there was still some room for improvement. After the game, the Ignis coach, Vittorio Tracuzzi, approached me, saying how impressed he had been by the play of Stan McKenzie, our guard-forward swingman and by far the best player on the team. He asked me if I would be interested in transferring McKenzie's rights to his team.

I wanted to agree for several reasons. I was just starting out in the tour business and the good will of a man like Borghi would be invaluable in the future for setting up games all over Europe. Also, it seemed a fine opportunity for Stan, who was an intelligent fellow and would enjoy living in Italy. And when Tracuzzi said that Ignis would pay Stan $20,000 a year—about the minimum salary in the NBA in 1966—I knew I had to work it out. There was no way I could justify keeping Stan around, playing for only a small per diem, when he had a chance like this. I mentioned it to him and he was just as enthusiastic as I thought he would be.

Still, there would be the cost of replacing Stan on the tour, particularly that of flying another player over from the United States. I brought this up and Tracuzzi agreed to foot the bill. What did I think was a reasonable amount? I said six hundred, thinking of the dollar amount of a transatlantic air fare. He replied that six hundred thousand lira would be fine. I had already made a profit of $400.

Before closing the deal, however, I said I would want to discuss it with Borghi. I had spent enough time in Italy to know that such matters are not handled coach to coach, but owner to owner. As a matter of principle—and ego—I would have to meet with the boss. Tracuzzi arranged it for the next day.

"We want Stan McKenzie to play on our team," said Borghi, who met me with great pomp and ceremony in his luxurious plant offices. "We recognize he is a fine player and that he will be a great loss for you. I understand that the replacement expense has been agreed upon. Now, what will you want for yourself?"

For *myself?* I could scarcely believe what I was hearing. I wanted to excuse myself and go out for a long walk to let the implications of what he was saying sink in, but there wasn't time for that. There was only one way to give myself enough time to think it over: stall. Luckily, my experience as coach of the Italian national team had taught me that this wouldn't seem out of the ordinary. Nothing ever gets done quickly in Italy, where bargaining is almost a national pastime.

So, while Borghi tried to get me to name a price, I made small talk or said nothing at all, trying to figure things out. At that time, the transfer of players from one team to another in Europe was not uncommon, but only in the last decade or so has it developed into something similar in extent to the buying and selling of players by American professional sports teams. Often, a lower-division team will have on its roster a young player who attracts the attention of an upper-division team. All parties recognize that the player's original club, having trained and developed him, has an equity in him and deserves some sort of compensation for giving him up.

But I was in no way responsible for the development of Stan McKenzie. If he had not been a good player, he would not have been on my team. All I had done was bring him to Europe. I didn't have the slightest idea what that was worth. Until that moment, it hadn't occurred to me that it was worth anything.

As Borghi tried to pin me down, I tried to deflect him. He asked me what I thought was a fair price. I told him I agreed in principle to giving up Stan if we could arrive at just compensation. He asked me what it would cost to find another player of Stan's caliber for my team. I complimented him on his magnificent plant and on the great contribution he had made to sports in his country.

As this went on, it was clear to me that Borghi was enjoying the negotiations almost as much as they were making me uncomfortable. They love to talk about *furbo* in Italy, which, freely translated, means "clever." I'm sure Borghi thought I was just trying to out-*furbo* him when I was trying only not to blow the whole thing.

"You Scots are like the Genovese," he said. Merchants from Genoa are considered by the Italians to be the best traders in the country. "And you are driving a hard bargain." I would have laughed if I hadn't been so nervous; I wasn't doing any bargaining at all. Finally, he saw he was going to have to make the first move.

"I can't spend as much time on this as I would like to, Mr. McGregor," he said. "Would you accept five million lira for the transfer?"

I'm sure I must have gulped. Five million lira was $8,000. A day earlier, I had been thrilled at the prospect of making $1,000 to cover the cost and trouble of finding a new player. I recovered fast enough to say, "I would like to open up a line of communication with you so that we can do business in the future and, in order to do this, I will make this exceptional price for Stan McKenzie."

The transaction worked out well for Stan, who remained in Italy for several seasons, after which he came back and played in the NBA for a time. And it worked out well for Borghi because Stan helped his team remain the top one in Italy. But it worked out best of all for me because from that moment until this I have been in a new business.

The presence of American players on the rosters of European club teams was nothing really new. After the war, the Belgians in particular, and the French, Germans and Italians to a lesser extent, had used players from the United States on their teams. Most often, these were American soldiers stationed in Europe. Army teams often played against club teams in the countries where they were stationed, and the clubs would sometimes invite the best American players to join them on weekends or during off-duty hours.

About the time I stumbled into sending McKenzie to Ignis Varese, several forces were converging to change this small-scale temporary situation—which had been the norm during my first stay in Italy a decade before—into a major, well-organized and lucrative system. One word sums it all up: boom.

The postwar Italian economic recovery took longer to get started than those that took place in Germany and Japan, but by the early 1960s, there was a large increase both in the amount of money available and in the number of people who had a lot of it. Many of the new Italian millionaires liked the prestige that owning a sports team offered, just as wealthy Texans enjoy having professional football teams in their portfolios. The Italian soccer teams, which had the most prestige, were unavailable, but basketball had recently gained a strong hold. Its speed and grace seemed to appeal to the Italian temperament.

All over the country, people with new fortunes began investing in basketball teams. Italy provided fertile ground for this phenomenon. There were dozens of cities with populations of over

50,000 and, unlike Rome or Naples or Florence—where so much was happening that there was no excitement about a comparatively new sport without any real tradition—a smaller city could identify immediately with a basketball team bearing its name. Soon, there were modern new arenas being built all over Italy.

Lately, corporate sponsorship has made an important contribution to the growth of basketball in Italy and in the rest of Europe. In 1968, to show how things have changed, I took a Gulf team to the Netherlands, where they made us take off our shirts because no commercial sponsorship was permitted. Today, every club team in the country is sponsored and the names of the sponsors are mentioned in the press all the time.

The second factor in the Italian basketball boom was the rise of television and its appetite for sports to fill up air time. Basketball televises extremely well because of its limited playing area, and the sport quickly became one of the most popular attractions of Italian television. The national sports press jumped on the bandwagon, giving basketball a lot of valuable free publicity alongside the voluminous soccer coverage.

These factors made basketball grow far too rapidly in Italy for the supply of home-grown players to fill the demand. It was clear that if the sport was to prosper, athletes from other countries would have to be commandeered. The Italian public seemed to have no real objection to this. Foreign players certainly did not hamper the growth of basketball the way the widespread use of Europeans and Latin Americans slowed the development of soccer as a spectator sport in the United States until recently. Then came the turning point, the catalyst that got the Italian basketball boom really started. Bill Bradley came to Italy.

In the early 1960s the former Princeton star had just finished his senior year and had gone to Oxford as a Rhodes scholar. The president and the coach of the Simenthal club in Milan, Adolfo Bogancelli and Cesare Rubini, signed him to a contract. These two Italians had modelled their roles after those of soccer officials in their country, which went a long way toward establishing the professionalism and legitimacy of club basketball in Italy. But nothing they ever did was as important as bringing Bradley to Italy.

Because of his ability and personality, Bradley immediately became a great favorite, and the arrival of an American television network in Italy to transmit his games back to the United States had a profound effect. Bradley's presence seemed to make the Italians eager to acquire topflight Americans for their teams. What happened in Italy was not lost on the rest of Europe.

The mid-1960s may have been the golden age for American basketball players. The ABA had just been formed and had entered into a bidding war with the NBA. This not only drove salaries up out of sight, but also gave jobs to players who would not have made the pros only a year or two previously. And the European basketball boom provided jobs for many more Americans. The year I sent Stan McKenzie to Ignis Varese, I used only twenty-two players on my tour and found jobs in Europe for two or three of them. Within two years, I was up to eighty players and was placing almost every one of them.

The pay in Europe is far from what it is in the NBA. With the exception of two or three of the top clubs, European teams will not compete with the United States for the best players. They go after the top ones in their salary range. Today, Real Madrid and Ignis Varese may go as high as $60,000 or $70,000, but the million-dollar contracts that the NBA offers its top stars are out of the question.

However, it is important to bear in mind that the salary a player receives in Europe bears little relation to its equivalent in this country. For one thing, the top first-division clubs in Europe have a long list of extras—they call them "perks"—that can add up to a lot. Players often get free apartments, cars, trips home and more. Also, the money they do make goes a lot farther than it does here. The first $30,000 is exempt from U.S. taxes. And in a country like Italy, a player pays taxes at a rate of only thirteen percent on one-third of his income. In other words, if he is making $60,000, he pays thirteen percent of $20,000, or only $2,600.

It must also be remembered that all the players in Europe are officially amateurs. Everybody knows that they are full-time players and getting paid on that basis, but the fiction of amateurism is maintained so that they will remain eligible for the Olympics. Much of their salary is officially listed as expenses, which are non-taxable. It is easy to see how a player in Europe might be doing as well as an NBA player making twice his salary.

There can be problems, though, that are not common in the United States. I have seldom run into any out-and-out dishonesty, but sometimes there is trouble when you deal with clubs that are not financially sound. A club president who needs a big year at the box office just to break even may take a chance on bringing in an American player in the hopes that he will draw crowds. But if things don't work out, the president may be ousted—this happens often in Europe—and the new regime may decide not to honor all the debts he incurred. The American player can go to court, but the legal system in some countries is complex and slow-moving, and the protection offered foreigners is not always what it should be. Also, the player is legally an amateur and not always given the same rights as a salaried worker. So it may not pay to stay in the country for months, trying to collect.

Still, many American players have had long and rewarding careers in Europe and some have married girls in the countries where they were playing, remaining there when they retired from basketball. The smart ones have learned the language and the customs and used their salaries and popularity to set themselves up in business. Many of them actually have done better than their counterparts who went into the NBA.

A lot of players do return to NBA careers, however, and more and more the pro scouts are beginning to realize that they may be able to find as many good American players in Europe as they can in the colleges. Very often, a player is still unfinished when he leaves school, and the experience he gets in Europe may be just what he needs to turn him into an NBA-caliber player. Over the years, I have recommended perhaps twenty players to the NBA and ABA on the basis of a European performance. Willie Norwood, Steve Hawes, Jim Fox and Kim Hughes are among them. In 1976, I sent Robin Jones to Portland, where he became a very useful backup center to Bill Walton on the team that won the NBA title. Jones was still a substitute at St. Louis University when he graduated and almost completely unknown. In fact, he got to Europe on his own and I first saw him in France. I could see he was coming on, not at all uncommon for big players who often develop late.

My touring teams have also included players who have gone on to the professional ranks. In the early days, players would often use the tour to prepare for the NBA season. This was fine with me then, but from the moment I sent Stan McKenzie to Ignis Varese, everything changed.

CHAPTER **16**

The Lonesome Guard

THE DISCOVERY that there was a market for the players I brought over to Europe had a profound effect on the makeup of my touring teams. During the first few years, I had the normal complement of players: two centers, four forwards and four guards. But I soon found that the biggest demand overseas was for centers. There just were not that many big players abroad, particularly not in Western Europe, and those who were there were not very skilled.

I began building my teams to meet the demand. It was not long before the Gulf All-Stars were composed of nine centers and a guard. The only reason the lone little man got in there was that somebody had to bring the ball down the court.

It made for interesting basketball and there was a lot more involved than passing, shooting and defense. I called it economic basketball when I explained it to the team. The biggest man on the club was stationed in the pivot; it became everybody else's job to get the ball in to him. The purpose of this was to make him look as good as possible until a club team picked him up. Then somebody else moved in under the basket and he got the ball. And so on, until everybody had a job and had been replaced by a new arrival from the United States. This could be frustrating for all the other big guys, reduced to passing the ball after years of playing under the basket and scoring thirty points a game. Occasionally, there would be a break from this routine in one of two ways.

A European team would ask to borrow one of our players to see how he fit in. This was common practice and I encouraged it because it meant the club team was very interested. Being the only big guy on a team once again seemed to have a liberating effect; invariably, the player on loan would have his best night of the tour against us. This was fine with me, as it helped move players along faster. In fact, we often tried to make him look good, as surreptitiously as possible.

Or, every once in a while, when we were playing a team not in the market for a center, we varied things a little and went to our famous four-post offense. It was quite a sight, what with four big guys taking turns popping in and out of the pivot and passing off to each other under the basket, while the poor lonesome guard stood outside and tried to keep from getting run over. It might seem as if we were sacrificing speed, but actually some of the big guys could move around pretty well and I honestly think they began to enjoy this type of basketball. They were being asked to pass the ball and think about what they were doing, rather than just shoot on offense and hustle down to get in position for the rebound on defense.

It was not difficult to find all the centers I needed for the tour. Many of them had actually been forwards in college. When you are six feet nine and on a team with a good seven-footer, you move quickly to the side of the court if you want to play. A lot of my draftees, in fact, didn't really know how to play in the middle and I would often have to hold a cram course. It must have looked odd to see me telling players a foot or more taller than I was how to play the pivot.

The bona fide centers were easy to find, too. By the time a player is a sophomore in college, he has usually reached his full height, so, if I could spot a center early, I would have several years to see how he developed. I also learned that the best place to find an underrated center is on a team with a high-scoring guard. He usually spends most of his time rebounding and passing off to the gunner, which is excellent training for a big man, and he usually gets almost no press attention. Art Kenny of Fairfield College and Gerhardt Schreur of Arizona State were two unheralded centers who had fine careers in Europe. Kenny was a nineteenth-round NBA draft choice and Schreur was not drafted at all.

Since I needed only one guard, I could afford to be choosy and I had to be. The ability to pass, dribble and shoot might have been enough for some coaches, but I required much more. The playmaker almost always became my team manager, trainer, assistant coach and confidant. He had to be smart and loyal, and he had to understand that no matter how good a player he was his chances of catching on with a European team right away were much smaller than were those of the centers. For one thing, the demand was not as great. For another, I needed him.

The guard also had to understand that I wanted him to do everything on the court except shoot. He was to put the ball up five times a game—just enough to give the opposing defenses something to think about—and no more. Ken Grant was my all-time perfect guard. He must have played 500 games for me, taken five shots in every one and made four of them.

Sometimes it was enough to break a guard's heart. In 1976, I brought over Jim Lee, a fine guard from Syracuse. He was a great shooter, and only the fact that he was just a wee bit slow kept him from making the NBA. After I saw him work out and make shots from all over the court, I told him the job was his and that he was the best shooter I had ever coached. Shoot all you want, I told him. That's what practice is for. At first, he thought I was kidding, but when we got to Europe, Jim followed my directions completely. I couldn't help but notice that when he did shoot, however, he never missed. So gradually during the tour, I would say, "Well, maybe you'd better shoot just a little more." He did and still he almost never missed. When he did, we asked for a new ball.

But if the guards didn't get to shoot much, they soon learned that if they followed orders they were guaranteed a spot on the tour as long as they wanted it. Players like Ken Grant, Fran O'Hanlon, Nelson Isley, Carmen Calzonetti, Bill Sweek and Billy De Angelus were with me for several years; most of them wound up playing and even coaching in Europe. By being around so long, they had a lot of time to make contacts. By being so useful to me they got good recommendations when I found adequate replacements.

In placing players in Europe, I soon learned to be aware of the likes and dislikes of the various teams. It did no good to say that Player A was better than Player B if Player A was six feet eight and Player B was a seven-footer, when the team was looking for somebody really big. Many European teams were hung up on size beyond all reason. I am convinced there are teams that would not take Dave Cowens because he is only six feet eight and never mind that he is one of the best centers in the game. That is why the bigger a player is, the closer a look I'm willing to take at him. If I can say a guy is seven feet tall, I know I can get a team to give him a tryout no matter how slow or clumsy he is.

The same sort of irrationality seems to exist with regard to black and white players. There are some countries that like to have American blacks on their club teams. The Swedes are naturally a very curious people and, having no black population of their own, are simply fascinated by black athletes. But even within a country, there are differing prejudices, both positive and negative.

Some European teams favor blacks and others favor whites; very often they seem to switch preferences from year to year. It seems to depend on the club's most recent experience. One team gets a white player, decides he's not tough enough and the next year goes for a black. Another team gets a black, decides he's a pain in the neck and then goes for a white. A third team gets a white player it likes and comes back for another. And a fourth team likes the black player it has and wants another. There's nothing so malignant in this type of prejudice, but it's just as silly as other kinds, I think.

If the makeup of my teams changed radically after the Stan McKenzie episode, so did the purpose of the tour. No longer was it to find sponsor money or a guarantee from a club team or a share of the television cut, though I never gave up those sources of income. Transferring players to European teams became my prime mission in life. The tour now centers around the availability of new players. We start in March, with the boys who got out of college the previous June and didn't make the pros. After that much inactivity, they're usually eager to play again.

In early June, there's a whole new wave of players. The NBA draft is held then and I get in touch with the athletes I am interested in who were drafted in low rounds. I don't waste time with the top choices who will try to stay in the United States where the most money is. I still have plenty to choose from and I don't mind taking a few players who want to try out for the NBA in the fall, despite the disappointment of being drafted late. Very often, a solid offer of $20,000 or $30,000 a year from a European club changes their minds about even wanting to go to an NBA training camp.

Then in the fall, after the first wave of NBA cuts, I start to get some big names. For every rookie who makes the NBA, a veteran is cut. Faced with the loss of his $100,000-plus salary, many a longtime pro looks to Europe.

In the fall of 1976, I got a call from David Wolf, who wrote Connie Hawkins' book, *Foul*. Hawkins had just been cut by the Los Angeles Lakers and finally had run out of teams to play for in the NBA. The settlement of his lawsuit against the league, for blackballing him on phony gambling allegations, had left him with a healthy income for many years, but Wolf said Hawkins still wanted to play. I guess the conversation got off on the wrong foot when I said we already had a sponsor. Wolf didn't seem to think that was funny.

Actually, I was most concerned about Hawkins' ability. He might have assumed his name alone would be enough to get him a lucrative job in Europe, but I thought differently. My attempts to ferret out information from Wolf were not very successful, though.

McGregor: How old is Connie?

Wolf: He's in great shape.

McGregor: How much did he play last year?

Wolf: He really wants to go to Europe.

McGregor: Tell him to get an Amateur Basketball Association of the USA card, reinstating him as an amateur. It costs up to fifteen hundred dollars to regain your virginity, you know.

Wolf (finally I have him asking questions): Can he make fifty thousand over there?

McGregor (enjoying his new role in the conversation): How old is Connie?

Wolf (refusing to give up and getting in a good one): Old enough to be an amateur again.

Finally, I decided that the risk of handling Hawkins was just too great. A team that signed him on the basis of his reputation would blame me if he flopped. Very recently, though, he went to Italy on his own. I will be interested to see how he does there and if I made a mistake. That's the chance I always take.

Among other players who think they can walk into jobs in Europe at high salaries are some who nearly make the NBA and figure Europe is a cinch. In 1976, a quality high-scoring guard from a Big Eight school—I won't mention his real name because he's still active—graduated. He was a fine player who won a lot of games for his team and was very close to an NBA job. But coming close did not get him a contract and he knew there would be another wave of college graduates in 1977. He decided he had better go to Europe. One day I was at home in Portland when the telephone rang.

"This is Charlie Gunner's agent," a voice said. "I hear you're the man who can do it in Europe."

"I place players in Europe, yes," I said.

"Well, Charlie would be interested in going to Europe, but, of course, he'd want fifty or sixty thousand dollars."

"I can understand that. I'd like to go to Europe myself for fifty or sixty thousand, and so would a lot of other people. If he's serious about going to Europe and he wants to know what he might be able to make, have him call me sometime when he's got his feet on the ground."

A few days later, the telephone rang again.

"This is Charlie Gunner's agent," a voice said.

"Didn't we talk the other day?" I said.

"No, no, Charlie was tied in with some fellow who didn't know much about the situation, but I know you're the man in Europe and you can get Charlie a good job over there. What can you get for him? Thirty thousand? Twenty-five thousand?"

"Look. I think Charlie's a fine player, very close to NBA caliber. But the demand in Europe is for centers. You tell him that if he's interested in knowing exactly what the situation is, he should call me."

The truth is, I could have called Charlie directly—I'm sure all his would-be agents ditched him as soon as they found out he wasn't about to come into the big money—any time after these conversations and told him he was welcome to join my tour. I would pay his expenses, give him an opportunity to show his stuff and maybe, if he was lucky, he would get a few months' work at the rate of $8,000 or $9,000 a year. But I didn't, because I already had my guard for the year.

Usually, my choices of players to take on the tour work out fairly well. Since I have to pay for my errors out of my own pocket, they had better. Of course, we all make mistakes. On my first Gulf tour, we played in Belgium against a team that had Jim Fox. There had been some interest in him in the NBA, but I couldn't see why, not after his performance against us. Shortly after that game, I was talking to an NBA scout who asked how Fox had looked. I believe my exact words were, "If he ever plays a minute in the NBA, I'd really be surprised." Fox came home and played ten years.

Another mistake. I once wrote a letter to John Wooden at UCLA, asking if he knew of any big men who might want to go to Europe. He wrote back immediately and said he had a big, strong fellow named John Ecker who he thought could play anywhere. I looked at Ecker's statistics. He had averaged two points and one rebound per game, which is a lot less than it takes to get me excited. What I didn't take into account, however, was that Ecker had played behind Sidney Wicks and Curtis Rowe, the two best forwards ever to play together at UCLA. Ecker simply hadn't been able to get into a game. And Wooden, it turned out, was giving it to me straight. Ecker was a fine, smart player. He went to Germany, had a brilliant career, married an Olympic skier and became one of the most popular Americans in the country—all without any assistance from me. Worse still, he became a sort of clearinghouse for UCLA players interested in playing in Germany, which cuts into the business of you-know-who. It will be a long time before I take the words of John Wooden lightly again.

Generally, however, my mistakes are not the players I leave home, but those I take. In 1976, I brought Rick Suttle to Europe. He was six feet ten, had been All-Big Eight at Kansas, a fourth-round NBA pick and looked very good in the NBA's Summer Pro League in Los Angeles, almost good enough to make the league. But when he first joined us, he was terrible. He just couldn't seem to hold onto the ball, and his attitude was not the best either.

When the tour got to Paris, I took him aside and said, "Rick, I'm going to lend you to the other team tonight. Let's see if you can do better against us than you've been doing for us."

All he did was score fifty-two points, which made the Paris team very interested in him. Its officials asked to try him out for two or three more games. If it worked out, they would pay him $20,000 and a car. Rick was willing and I certainly was, so we left him behind. A week later, he was back and would say only that he hadn't been able to come to terms. This seemed strange to me because we had already agreed on a price. I called the Paris club president.

"He's a fine player," I was told, "but we couldn't agree on the conditions."

"What the hell?" I said. "We already had an agreement."

"Well, we were all set to sign, but when we started talking

about the car, he found out it had a stick shift and he wouldn't take it."

"You mean to tell me he turned down a job like this because he wanted an *automatic shift?*"

"Believe it or not, that's what happened and, frankly, if he's going to be that way about something like that, we're afraid of what might come up later."

"I don't blame you," I said.

Normally, a story like that would get around European basketball circles in a hurry, but somehow we got to Italy ahead of it and managed to get Rick a job with a team there. In fact, he got even more money than he would have made in Paris—$30,000. I think he bought his own car.

Then there is my Hank Simenkowski story. It's been so long now that I can laugh about it, although that was far from my original reaction. Hank was a good big player at Villanova, a high NBA draft choice at one time. When he didn't make the pros, he looked me up.

The team was already in Europe, so I told him to fly over to Rome. Somebody would meet him at the airport, I said, but in case of a mix-up, I gave him my office number. As it turned out, the people who were supposed to meet him got tied up in traffic, which can be horrendous around the airport. And it was Sunday, so nobody was at the office. Hank, finding himself stranded in a foreign country where nobody could pronounce his name, did what anybody would do. He went home. His one hour in Rome cost me $1,000 and set the all-time record for the shortest stay of the tour.

No, I take that back. There was one player who didn't make it as far as Hank did. In fact, I would have forgotten all about him if he weren't in a team picture I still have. One year, I held my tryouts at Kutscher's, the famous resort in New York's borscht belt. Dallas Thornton, an effective big player who later went to the Harlem Globetrotters, made the team.

The night before we were to leave for Brazil, I set a curfew one of the few times in my career. We had to catch an early plane, take a long flight and play an important game as soon as we disembarked. I knew the players wouldn't get much rest on the plane so I asked everybody to get in early. Everybody did, except Dallas Thornton. I kicked him off the team. Thus, his whole career is right there in that team picture.

My mail brings me many applications from players. I never get any decent leads this way, but I do get some laughs.

(*Written by hand*) Man, I can do it all. I would have been an All-American but the man didn't go for my life-style. I'm a winner and I want to play in Europe. I've played with Monroe, Robertson and Chamberlain and they all say I can do it all. . . . (I have never heard of him, but I know he's a guard. There was one guy I almost took because of his sense of humor. He had a letterhead printed up, reading, "Basketball's Unknown Man.")

(*Written by an attorney*) We represent Joe Dunk, whom you have undoubtedly heard about. He has a no-cut offer from several NBA clubs, but would rather play in Europe. . . . (I have never heard of him, either, and when you consider that I read basketball rosters for pleasure and basketball magazines to my ten-year-old daughter as bedtime stories, you will realize this takes some doing.)

(*Written by a coach*) I want to recommend for the European leagues Tom Tipin, who played for us for four years and was named honorary captain and most inspirational player. He won the Tipin Cup, donated by his father, the chairman of the board of trustees. He didn't have great stats, but this was due to his unselfish play. Anything you can do to help him will be appreciated. By the way, how are coaching opportunities in Europe?

CHAPTER **17**

Love and the Passport Office

NOT LONG AFTER I became deeply involved in the placement of American players on foreign teams, I began to see that it wasn't going to be quite as easy as it had seemed. The demand was great, all right, and the supply of players back home was virtually inexhaustible; but there were difficult problems to be solved, nevertheless.

For one thing, I wasn't entering a field that was totally un-regulated. Most countries had rules governing the participation of foreign players on their teams, complicated enough to be worthy of a chapter or two in a book on international law. One difficulty was that these rules differed from country to country and even within countries. Another was they were constantly be-ing changed.

In most European countries, for instance, first-division teams were allowed to use two foreign players. Italian teams were al-lowed only one. This rule, however, applied only to club-team play. In inter-European competition, each team was allowed two foreign players. So some Italian teams carried an extra player around just to use in games against other countries.

In France, teams were allowed two foreigners, but often carried three in case a player was injured. But recently, lower-division teams in France and Sweden had had their foreign quotas cut from two to one, which affected me because suddenly another forty to fifty American players were on the European market.

There was no limit to the number of foreign players allowed on a team during the popular Italian summer tournaments. And, since many European players often took vacations during this period, the various continental club teams used these tournaments to appraise American players they were interested in for the up-coming season. There have been times, in fact, when my touring team would meet a club representing Simenthal or Ignis Varese, whose only Italian member was the coach. Still, these teams represented Italy and we were the foreigners, so all through the game the fans would cheer them on—"Ee-tal-*ya!* Ee-tal-*ya!*"— and boo us.

Patriotism and national pride constantly came into play in this area. One faction in most countries recognized that the influx of American players raised the level of basketball, brought out more fans and generally increased interest in the sport. But some journalists and officials felt the presence of Americans hindered the development of local players. This has remained a question without a real answer and one that will be debated for years.

But for all the rules and regulations aimed at limiting the number of foreign players, there were probably as many attempts to circumvent them. The most ingenious of them all didn't take long to surface. If teams were to be restricted in the number of Americans permitted, why not simply naturalize the Americans? That way, there would be no limit at all; everybody would be European. How could you discriminate against, say, a bona fide Frenchman —who had the passport to prove it—simply because he was born and raised in Cleveland?

In a short time, players from the United States began appearing on teams all over Europe carrying the passports of France, Spain, Belgium, Italy, Greece and other countries. Naturalization regulations were not very stringent in many of these countries and a player who was really determined could generally find his way around any difficulties.

The easiest way to obtain French citizenship, for instance, was to marry a Frenchwoman. I know of several players who, tired of competing each year for one of the two spots on their teams reserved for foreigners, got married instead. It's hard to say if these marriages were made in the throes of true love or in the passport office.

French officials did their best to combat this situation by adopting a rule barring naturalized players, including those who had wed their way onto team rosters. This sent shock waves through some new marriages, I'm sure. But there are lawyers in France, too, and, when the players appealed, the new regulation was thrown out by the courts. The course of true love doubtless was unimpeded after that.

A French newspaperman once studied the naturalization figures for a particular year and made an interesting discovery. People from all over the world had become French citizens: Algerians, Eastern Europeans, Latin Americans and so on. But the only new Frenchmen who had anything in common were the twenty-four Americans who had switched nationalities. They were all basketball players.

Nor was this strictly a French phenomenon. The Swiss passport is said to be the most difficult in the world to obtain. Not if you are a basketball player, it turns out. And the starting five on the national team of the Netherlands one recent year were all Dutch-Americans. The question of who is a Jew, and therefore entitled to Israeli citizenship, is one that is the subject of the most heated, hair-splitting debates in that country. The fate of the government has hung in the balance more than once when this emotional topic has arisen. Yet not long ago, a black American and a Mormon from Brigham Young University were members of the Israeli club championship team. And an Israeli team recently won the European club championship because it had seven Americans on its roster while poor Ignis Varese, the Italian champion, only had three.

Then there was the plight of Corky Bell, who became a Belgian citizen in order to remain on a club team in that country.

One of the responsibilities of Belgian citizenship is a tour of duty in the army. Corky didn't mind too much because basketball players in the Belgian army do the same thing they do in the U.S. army: They play basketball. But when he arrived for his military training, he found that the army, like the country, was split down the middle between the French-speaking population and those who spoke Flemish. Corky didn't speak either language. He had the distinction of being the entire English-speaking contingent of the Belgian army.

Other players had the best of both worlds. Ted Christopher, from Northeastern University, was Greek enough to play on the national team of that country, but American enough to be a professor at Pierce American University in Athens. And to be well paid for both jobs.

My favorite entrant in the switched-nationality sweepstakes may well be Carlos Mina. He was born in the United States, but his father was born in Mexico and his grandfather was born in Italy. Carlos played at Long Beach State, but suddenly he showed up on the Mexican team at the Pan-American Games. There was even talk that he would make the Mexican Olympic team. But when he came to me and I found out about his Italian grandfather, I told him to get a passport from that country. He has played in Italy ever since.

At any rate, I got into the ancestry business just about as deeply as Alex Haley did. It was quite a jump from recruiting players on the basis of their ability to checking out where their great-grandfathers were born.

There was another aspect to transferring players in Europe that I had to get used to quickly—the kickback. Often, the coach or general manager of a team in the market for a player would let it be known that the deal required something in it for him. The first time this happened, I decided that it was none of my business. If the man asking for the kickback wanted to rob his own team owner, that was his concern. All I asked was that I be informed far enough in advance to be able to add the kickback to my fee. I certainly didn't want it to come out of my pocket.

Once, when I had a very good European sponsor lined up for my tour, the key man in the deal approached me at the last minute and mentioned a kickback. The sponsor was to pay $50,000 for an eight-month tour, and the intermediary wanted $10,000 to set it up. I wouldn't have been averse to paying it if I had known about it ahead of time. I would have simply set my price at $60,000 and everybody would have been happy. So I turned down the deal on the high moral grounds that I hadn't made provisions for the kickback earlier.

If the problems of player limitations and kickbacks were ones that I hadn't been ready for when I began this operation, there was one difficulty that I could see coming right from the start. This was too promising a business to have to myself for long. I began to wonder how long it would be before others would see its money-making potential. Soon, I had my answer: not long enough.

It began in Belgium, where the sport had always been well organized. Instead of dealing through me, several of the Belgian clubs simply got directly in touch with American coaches and players. Very quickly, an agent would become involved and he and the team would strike up an agreement. Finding people to play in Europe was easy if you were an agent. You had only to call a player not quite good enough for the NBA and offer to represent him. It was finding the European club for him to join that took time and money because of the distance involved. Once a European team or league offered to place the players the agent found, the job became a lot easier.

Soon countries where I had once had a monopoly—Italy in particular—became extremely competitive markets. Over the years, there have been two or three principal competitors who have given me the most headaches, while a few new ones seem to pop up every year. Also, unkindest cut of all, some of my former players go into competition with me.

One of these was Glendor Torain, who played at Dayton, then went on the tour and wound up with a lengthy career in France and Belgium. He liked Belgium well enough to want to stay there, so he took a look at the market and came up with an ingenious plan. He saw that the third- and fourth-division teams, the equivalent of the lower minor leagues in baseball, were widely ignored by player merchants like myself. In the first place, I didn't have enough players to supply any teams other than the top ones. Also, I couldn't make much money from lower-division teams because the fees they paid were too low.

But Glendor saw a wide-open market in the lower divisions, composed of about 200 teams. If he could supply, say, fifty players a year and make $500 on each, he could earn a decent living. As soon as he got started, we struck up a little deal. He left the upper-division teams to me and I sent him an occasional player for his teams.

As for the agents back in the United States, they have one big advantage over me when it comes to dealing with the big-name players. They can represent them in negotiations with the NBA and, if the players don't make it, then try to make a European deal. To players, this often seems an impressive arrangement, but the fact is that many of these agents have no experience in the foreign market and come to me for help. So the player may wind up paying an agent's fee for work I would do at no cost to him.

This is the big difference between me and most of my competitors. The agent works for the player and is paid by him. I work for the team and am paid by it. There are advantages and disadvantages to both arrangements. The agent can tell the player, "Look, McGregor is working for the club. I'm looking out for your interests. So I'm going to get you a better deal than he will."

I, on the other hand, can say honestly, "I have the widest contacts in Europe and know all the teams that might need a player like you. In fact, I'll take you on tour and show you to several clubs, whereas an agent can only set up a tryout. Also, the club pays me; you don't. Why pay an agent five or six thousand dollars to do what I do for free?"

I have one other major handicap that an agent doesn't have. I am a player merchant, but I am also a tour promoter and in many cases I work in both capacities with the same people. If I make a bad deal for the club—that is, send it a player who doesn't work out or isn't worth the money—its officials aren't going to be very happy with me when I call and try to schedule a game for my touring team. I may well lose a night of revenue every future year. But if an agent sends a team a stiff, he has lost one club out of hundreds with which he can deal.

There have been occasions when I have worked with an agent in the United States. In fact, the most amazing negotiations I have ever been involved in took place in such a situation. They revolved around Jim McDaniels, who may have made as much money out of basketball as anyone who ever played the game. Or perhaps I should say hardly ever played the game.

McDaniels was a seven-footer who had the extreme good fortune to get out of college when the signing war between the NBA and the ABA was at its fiercest. He wound up signing an incredible contract with Seattle of the NBA, paying him something like $100,000 a year for eighteen years. But when he got to Seattle, he didn't play much. Finally, Bill Russell, a man with very high standards when it came to big centers, became the Seattle coach and cut him. McDaniels still had a lot of money coming, but he was also free to look around for another job.

Al Ross, one of the best agents in the business when it came to squeezing every possible dollar out of a team, came to me and asked if I could place McDaniels in Europe. I inquired in Italy and found three clubs that were extremely interested. One was in the city of Udine, another was in Bologna and the third was in Venice. I made it clear they would have to deal through Ross, who had offered me a small portion of his percentage. This wasn't the way I usually worked, but in this case I was willing to make an exception.

The Udine club was so anxious to sign McDaniels that the owner's son and the club treasurer asked me to fly to Los Angeles, where Ross had his office, and help them make their bid in person. Ross put on a magnificent performance. We would all be in his office when his secretary would come in, whisper something and hand him a telegram, which he would place conspicuously on his desk. A few minutes later, he would be buzzed and told a call had just come in from Venice. Ross would ask to be excused, leaving us to assume he was going to discuss McDaniels with the Venice team. Then one of the Udine people would sneak a peek at the telegram, which would be from Bologna. This went on for several days and Udine, which had set a limit of $50,000 on its bid for McDaniels, slowly kept raising the ante. Every time they were about to close the deal, there would be another telegram or phone call. In the end, they agreed to pay McDaniels $100,000, plus such perks as a villa, a car, performance bonuses and round trips to Italy for him and his family and even for Ross and his family, adding at least $15,000 or $20,000 to the package.

McDaniels went to Udine and, though he played pretty well, the team didn't improve in the standings. He was back home after one season. Amazingly, McDaniels fired Ross shortly afterwards. He claimed Ross wasn't doing a good job representing him.

On one other occasion I cooperated with someone else and seriously regretted it. In 1976, this person came to me, offering to find a sponsor for my summer tour of Italy and pay me $25,000 to supply the team. The idea of not having to hunt up a sponsor, which can be a frustrating, time-consuming business, appealed to me, and I agreed to give him anything over the $25,000 the sponsor would pay.

He went out and found an Italian wine company willing to pay $35,000 and soon he began to wonder why he should give any of it to me. If he recruited his own team, he thought, not only could he keep all the money, but he could also merchandise players to teams in Italy. So he got in touch with an agent in the United States who agreed to supply him with the players for a cut of the European transfer fees.

The moment I heard about this, it was war. By trusting him, I had stopped looking for a sponsor and was out the $25,000. He had to be taught a lesson. He had lined up a schedule for his team with tournament organizers in Italy, but I had been around long enough to know that there are always last-minute changes where these things are concerned. I was determined to cause a few. I went around to all the tournaments I had been competing in for years and said, "I'm willing to participate this year, but on one condition, that mine is the only American team."

"But this is an Olympic year," I was told. "It's hard to get teams because every country has a national team in training now. Our costs are going up and you're asking for more money again."

"Well, I think we can find a way to settle this," I said. "I'll play for *less* money, on the condition that no other American team is in the tournament."

In the end, my team played in twelve tournaments in Italy, his team only in four. And since he couldn't showcase his players, he couldn't place them all on the Italian teams. So he had to do what none of us can afford to do—fly players back home. I had twelve players and moved them all. He had twelve and moved only three.

In Chieti, in one of the tournaments that I had been unable to shut him out of, I was faced with a real dilemma. We had the strongest team by far, but a good Italian team, an important client over the years, asked me for the loan of Mike Stewart, a big man I had brought over from Santa Clara. I wanted to make a strong showing in the tournament to embarrass my rival, but I knew that, if Stewart played well for the Italians, I could expect a large transfer fee. And when they offered to *pay* me just to borrow Stewart for the tournament, all my good intentions flew out of the window.

The tournament started out well; we won the first game and my rival's team lost. But in the second game, we faced the Italian team. Mike played well against us and we lost by a point. My rival's team lost, too, but in the third game the two American teams met and we were beaten. I had been embarrassed by my own greed.

Both of us moved on to the next tournament and there I got my revenge. We met in a semifinal game, which was important because the finals were going to be televised. For a sponsor, this means the most of all. I told my players there would be a $25 bonus per man if we won, which we did. I found out later that my rival's sponsor was furious. I wonder how he felt when he learned the team he was paying for wasn't even in the next two tournaments because I had frozen it out.

As mad as I got at this rival, it was nothing compared to the time I really became angry at a competitor. This thief would go down to Times Square in New York, buy the Italian papers and read that such-and-such an American player had signed on with my tour. Then he would call up the player, introduce himself as my associate and tell him we had transferred his rights to a foreign team. The next thing I knew, the player was in Europe, but no longer on the tour, and my competitor had pocketed the transfer fee. He spent a whole summer transferring players I had supposedly signed. Needless to say, I stopped telling the Italian press whom I was bringing over with me. It took me a few years to get even, but when the time came, I was ready.

I was on the telephone to a club in Europe one day and brought up the name of a player who was a senior in college. Funny you should mention him, the club official said. We were just talking to your competitor, who says he represents him. That was great news for me. I called the player's college and said, "Look, there's an unscrupulous bastard running around Europe saying he represents one of your players. You know that NCAA rules say you can't sign with an agent while you're still playing in college. If this gets back to their investigators, your school will have to forfeit all its games. I just wanted to warn you."

Now, I knew my competitor had no signed deal with the player. Claiming he did was just a way to establish a relationship with the European club. But the mere claim was good enough for me. Soon, that college was bad-mouthing this fellow terribly, and his business dried up for quite some time. It couldn't have happened to a more deserving guy.

Not all of my competition comes from people in the business for the money. As the number of American players in Europe increases every year, so does the amateur job-placement rivalry I must face. Many players, out of the goodness of their hearts, try to get jobs for their friends and they are in excellent positions to do so. They hear about openings constantly. All they have to do is ask the club if there's any interest in a buddy and, if so, call him up and tell him to hurry on over. And the fellow who is making a living placing players in Europe finds himself in the position of the hooker on the street, complaining about all the girls who are giving it away.

Lately, my competition has come from an entirely new source. There are organizations in the United States willing to send teams on tour for non-financial purposes. Recently, a young guy in New York persuaded an American-Israeli sports committee to take a good team of Jewish players to Israel where he scheduled some games. On his way back, he stopped off at the Italian summer tournaments. I was able to limit his participation to just one or two tournaments, but I was worried when I found out he planned a repeat performance for the following year. Fortunately for me, he had some problems in Israel—some games were cancelled—and he lost money. He has since dropped out of sight.

No sooner had I fended off this fellow than I began to feel like the infidel fighting the legions of God on all sides. The Mormons came sailing through Italy one summer and now I have to contend with the religiously oriented Athletes in Action. This is a team of former college players who are extremely competitive in the United States, often beating college teams. Overseas, they play under the banner of Crusade for Victory. Luckily, they haven't entered the major Italian tournaments yet, but I expect that day will come soon. Since they have strong financial backing and great organizational strength, I expect them to be a real threat.

Teams like this erode my player talent pool as well as give me trouble in foreign tournaments. I'm thinking of returning to my days in Portland when I went to every church in town so I could play all the time. Only now, I'll do it to get players for my teams.

CHAPTER **18**

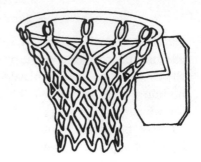

And Now, a Word from Our Sponsor

THINGS WENT SO WELL with Gulf as our sponsor during the first few years of the tour that it never occurred to me that the relationship would end. In the second year, we added a tour of Latin America and the publicity was tremendous. There was huge press and television coverage everywhere we went and it was clear that the company took great pride in us. Stories about the team were prominent in the Gulf house organs all over the world as well as in the corporate newspaper that came out of Pittsburgh.

Paul Sheldon told me that, at almost every board meeting, in the midst of discussions about which ships to buy and how the world price of oil was holding up, somebody was sure to ask, "How's the basketball team doing?" They got a kick out of bringing up our won-lost record in the midst of the profit statements.

Gulf's sponsorship was certainly the most lucrative I have ever had, giving me $70,000 the first year of the tour and $85,000 by the fourth year. Had I been running a tight ship the way I do today, I could have put quite a sum of money away. But it never occurred to me that we didn't have to stay in first-class hotels or live quite as high on the hog as we did. I suppose I developed a civil-service mentality, that it would go on forever.

Toward the end of the 1969 tour, I sent Paul what by then had become a routine letter about renewing for the following year. He called me from Pittsburgh, said he was going to be in London the following week and wanted me to meet him there. If there was one talent Paul had, it was dishing out bad news. He may be the only man I've ever met who can break your heart and make you feel good about it. Still, it hit me pretty hard when I found out why he had come to London.

"Jim, you've done a great job," he said, "and we've been pleased with you. But we feel that we've made our penetration into this sector of the public and now we want to sponsor some auto racing, which has an obvious tie-in with motor oil and gasoline."

There had been a change at the top of the company. A new executive vice president had been appointed, a specialist in foreign marketing who thought auto racing was a better way to advertise. My own feeling was that it would cost them twenty times as much to sponsor a racing team as a basketball team and the move was unlikely to produce any more publicity than we had been getting. But it was hard to deny the tie-in of auto racing with the sponsor's product. Besides, nobody had asked me. I thanked Paul for all he had done for me and went back out on the street again.

Since then, I've had half a dozen sponsors for various lengths of time and under various arrangements. But the hunt for sponsors has never ended since the day Gulf and I parted company.

In my dealings with sponsors, I wasn't prepared for the extent to which I had to cultivate them *after* we had signed an agreement. It wasn't enough just to acquire a sponsor; you had to hold onto him, as well. This took a lot of time and effort that wasn't always forthcoming on my part.

It's important, for instance, to keep the sponsor informed about what you're doing. You have to make him feel that he's part of the action. It sounds simple, but it was a constant problem. Take the matter of publicity. Our playing schedule wasn't arranged far enough in advance to forward the information to the sponsor's representative in most of the towns we visited. Which meant I had to deal with the press on my own. Which meant I had to cut out the local people. Which made them mad at me.

Then there was the question of tickets, a responsibility of the home club. I was never given any and I certainly wasn't about to buy any for the sponsors. This was a constant source of problems and misunderstandings. As a result, I often alienated the very people I needed the most. Generally, the local sponsors were independent businessmen, not just the representatives of a home office somewhere else. Thus, they had a great deal of power at contract-renewal time.

Often, we would arrive in a town to find that the sponsor had arranged some sort of marketing tie-in, of which I was unaware. He might want the players to make a public appearance or to give autographs at a local supermarket and he assumed that we were at his disposal. After a game the previous night, and a long trip, we weren't always thrilled by the plans made for us in advance.

The best sponsor I ever had in this respect was TWA. All the airline ever asked me to do was to wear its shirts and fly its planes. TWA had an overworked European advertising director whose instructions to me were simple: "I don't want to hear about you. I don't want to know about you. I just want you to go out and get a lot of press and don't bother me." My kind of guy.

We were a pretty good deal for him, too. TWA seldom gave us any money. We took out most of our business in trade. I could save as much as $20,000 a year in airline fares, but as far as TWA was concerned, we were just taking up seats that otherwise would have been empty.

The longest I ever spent with one sponsor was five years with Gillette, which backed us in Europe from 1971 to 1975. First, Gillette in Italy sponsored us in the games we played in that country. The next year, we picked up two or three more countries and for the last three years we were sponsored by Gillette in most of Europe. The problem was that Gillette had autonomous management, so I had to sell myself, country by country, all over Europe. There was an international coordinator, but he could only refer me to the various countries' headquarters. And I had to keep on wooing them because each contract covered only one year. Pretty soon, I was spending as much time chasing after

Gillette as I was recruiting and coaching my team. But they were paying me $400 a game for our 120-game schedule and, for $48,000, I was willing to do a lot of chasing.

Since Gillette is a manufacturer of men's toiletries, particularly shaving products, the company was absolutely consumed by the idea of neat appearance. It was selling good grooming and all that went with it, and there were times when this caused us problems. Since we played almost every night and travelled a large part of every day, it wasn't always possible to have uniforms laundered after each game. That bothered Gillette and as there seemed to be a local outlet for the company in just about every city in which we played, I was constantly hearing about it in phone calls.

"Coach McGregor! Why were your uniforms so dirty last night?" was the cry.

If there was anything calculated to send Gillette into a frenzy, it was the idea of beards. These were the 1970s, and very few people in the United States still made much of an issue over beards and long hair. And I have to admit, the new look didn't bother me as much as it once did. My Levi's-sponsored hippie team had mellowed me, I guess. But whenever a bearded player joined the team, I told him patiently who our sponsor was and that there was a no-beard clause in our contract. There was never any trouble about it. Except once.

We were in France and I had just transferred a player to a local club team. I sent for a man I knew about who was already in the country and told him to join us in Le Mans, where we had a game the following night. He showed up at the gym just at game time—wearing a full beard. The next day, two pictures of the game appeared in the local paper and it takes no imagination to guess who was in both of them. I expected an angry phone call and I wasn't disappointed.

"Coach McGregor!" the Gillette man shouted. "I want to call your attention to the clause in your sponsorship agreement that requires your players to be well-groomed, neat and clean-shaven."

"I'm more than aware of it," I said, "but this fellow just arrived. It would have been hard to shave him during a fast break.

You can be sure he'll be not only shaved but bleeding tonight."

The games I worried most about when Gillette was my sponsor were the televised ones. I did everything I could to make sure our uniforms were spotless, our shoes were squeaky-clean and everyone was shaven down to the nub. One night, we were in La Coruña, on Spanish national television, and everything seemed to be fine in the cleanliness department. Then the Spanish and American national anthems were played. The Spaniards stood like tin soldiers through both of them, but when I looked over at my boys, two of them were staring at the floor and playing with their jockstraps. I didn't have to look to know where the camera was pointing. I knew I could expect another phone call.

"Coach McGregor...!"

At one point in my hunt for sponsors, I wrote to Coca-Cola and Pepsi-Cola. Both companies have huge advertising budgets and both soft drinks are sold everywhere around the world. As far as I was concerned, this meant we were made for each other. I hoped one company would see it that way, too. I wasn't prepared for what happened, however. Both firms wrote to their offices in various countries, asking for reactions to sponsoring a basketball team. Coke got an affirmative reply from Greece. Pepsi got a yes from Formosa and the Philippines.

The idea of dividing my loyalties like this had never occurred to me. I had always had one sponsor for all or most of a tour and I had never had competing sponsors. But I saw no reason not to have a sponsor for just one or two countries; and with Coke in Greece and Pepsi in the Far East, well, there was half a world between, wasn't there?

Our arrival in Manila, after the games in Greece, astonished me. Clearly, Pepsi had pulled out all the stops. We were met at the plane by all the top officials of the company. We had a big press conference at the airport, drove through town in open cars with huge banners waving and were met at the hotel by another large crowd, including more reporters and photographers. I wondered if anybody since MacArthur had been given a more rousing welcome to the Philippines. After all the excitement, I decided to take a nap. In about an hour, I was awakened by a knock at the door.

It was a photographer from one of the local papers, with some pictures he wanted to show me. I started thumbing through them, seeing nothing unusual—just a bunch of players sitting around in the new Pepsi-Cola jackets and shirts handed out on our arrival. Great, I thought. The sponsor would love us. Then I saw, in the midst of all the pictures in which the word, "Pepsi," was prominently displayed, one jarring note. One of the players was wearing a Coke uniform shirt he had used in Greece. I knew exactly why the photographer had come.

"How much?" I asked.

He grinned. "Two hundred dollars."

I was in no position to argue. I was glad the crooked son of a bitch had brought the picture to me before showing it to anybody at his paper. We might have left the Philippines somewhat ahead of schedule and with a lot less ceremony.

There is nothing I'd like more than a nice, secure, long-term relationship with a sponsor, but eventually I realized it was never likely to be. There are several factors that work against it. For one thing, when I'm dealing with a corporation, everything boils down to selling myself and my concept to a man in a key position. He might be the sales director, the advertising manager, the head of the European division or the president of the company itself. Whoever he is, he almost always turns out to be a sports fan who likes the idea of a basketball team as part of his company's image.

The problem arises when a new man moves into the key position, which happens in business all the time. I have no guarantee that he will see sports in the same light as his predecessor. Even if he does, there is a psychological factor to deal with. A new man is supposed to have new ideas. Very often, he will change things just to establish his authority.

Then there is the fact that advertising—which is basically what I am providing—is so changeable. The tendency is to keep moving it around to reach different segments of the population. We've hit the basketball fan for a while; now, how about the soccer fan? How about the housewife? The teenager? And so on.

My most constant adversary is the advertising agency. Every large company has one, paying it fifteen percent of a total advertising billing. Except for the part I handle. I deal directly with the company. The result is, whatever money the company is spending on basketball is money the agency is not getting fifteen percent of. I'd be delighted to pay a percentage to an advertising agency if it could guarantee me a sponsor, but that's not the way it works. The agency sells the client to the medium, not the medium to the client.

It's true that I'm saving the company that fifteen percent, but agencies speak a very special language that is impressive to a company trying to decide how to spend its advertising dollar. Agencies use techniques and surveys to prove how a certain spot on a certain television show, or a certain ad in a certain magazine, has provided certain measurable results. There is simply no way that I can prove that my team wearing a Gulf shirt in the Italian summer tournament or that my team appearing on British television has induced drivers in either of those countries to buy No-Nox.

So I am constantly chasing sponsors. It's become a never-ending part of the business, but, frankly, I'm not as intense about it any more. At fifty-five, I'm not the same old Jim McGregor I was when the mother of invention was breathing down my neck all the time. I don't have the same hunger for recognition or the same pressing financial needs I once had, so I don't go after sponsors with the same drive.

Also, I no longer absolutely have to have a sponsor. Transferring players is the steadiest part of my business. In a sense, the foreign club teams are my real sponsors. It's much nicer when somebody picks up some or all of the expenses, but the most important thing is to keep the tour going.

That's why, in 1976, we travelled under the auspices of the most agreeable, charming, personable, cooperative sponsor I have ever had—Jim McGregor's International Basketball Camp.

PART THREE

On Tour

CHAPTER **19**

Europe on Ten Hollers a Day

T̲ʀᴀᴠᴇʟʟɪɴɢ ᴀʟᴏɴᴇ in Europe for any length of time can present problems. But making the arrangements and being constantly responsible for twelve to fifteen people generally borders on the hopeless. Getting around by train and plane is hard enough, but there have been many occasions when there was simply no other way but to drive. Sometimes, I wake up in a cold sweat just thinking about it.

The first year I took a team on tour, we used several station wagons. It was impossible to stay together and one of the cars almost always got lost or arrived late. The fact that none of us was familiar with driving in Europe didn't help, either.

Once in Naples, we arrived at a piazza, which can scare an American driver out of his wits. You drive around a central point until you come to the cross street you're looking for and then you turn off. On this occasion, the lead car turned left and headed clockwise, while the two cars following it went right. We almost had a three-car collision halfway around. This would have been remarkable, since there were several hundred cars in the piazza at the time and we came within inches of hitting only each other.

In 1968, a perfect solution to the driving problem presented itself. Or so it seemed at the time. The Gulf team started the tour in Sweden just about the time that country decided to get in step with most of the rest of Europe and begin driving on the right-hand side of the road. When this switch was made, all the buses in the country were suddenly obsolete. The doors being on the left, people would be stepping out of them right into traffic. It would have been expensive to modify these buses, so there were a lot of them available at very reasonable prices. I saw my chance and bought one, spending $4,000 for a bus that cost ten times that when new.

It was huge, built to accommodate sixty passengers, which meant that, after we took out many of the seats, there was plenty of room for every player to stretch out, as well as for all our luggage and a never-ending assortment of hitchhikers. I shouldn't say assortment, really. The hitchhikers we picked up all had one thing in common. They were female. There was a little toilet in the back of the bus and I spent most of my first few days of ownership congratulating myself for my foresight in buying it. This euphoria lasted right up until we took our first ride.

I was the driver on our maiden voyage. Being extra cautious, I looked around very carefully and adjusted the mirrors so I could get the best view possible out the back window, which seemed to be several miles away. When I had everything finally under control, I backed up slowly until I was clear of the car in front of me and began to pull forward. I had driven a short distance when I realized there was a large group of people in the street outside rushing madly after us.

I stopped and got out and only then did I realize that we were hauling an unexpected load—a little Fiat that now looked somewhat like an accordian. I had smacked into it when backing up and never even felt the impact. That was the end of my career as a chauffeur. No longer, I thought, would I recruit nine centers and one guard for my teams. From then on, it would have to be eight centers, one guard and one bus driver.

Luckily, there were several players on that particular team who could drive the bus. Dick Kolberg, a forward from the

University of California at Santa Barbara, had a license, and Stan Pelcher, who had played at Central Connecticut College, also had experience. But it was Ricardo Duarte, the star of my Peruvian team from years past, who really saved us in the bus department. Ricardo had had experience with buses in his own country since Latin America is where old buses go—not to die, but to live. They are patched up and kept running long after we Americans usually send them to the junkyard.

Ricardo had a magic touch, not only as a driver but also as a mechanic. He always seemed to be able to make the thing go with just a piece of wire. It wasn't really very smart to use one of my best players to urge the bus along for up to eight hours a day, after which he had to play basketball. Ricardo's performance began to suffer as the tour progressed, but he was our most valuable player because he could get us to where we were going.

Even with Ricardo at the wheel, the bus gave us trouble. It had half a dozen gears, but only a few of them ever seemed to work at any one time. It was extremely difficult to steer and, since it was so long and many of the European streets were so narrow, even the most routine turns became an adventure. Often, we made them by just shearing off the side of whatever object was in the way.

The older the city we were in, the more trouble we had. In parts of Italy, France and Spain, we would turn off a main drag and into a sidestreet, only to see it become narrower and narrower until we were hemmed in on all sides. There were times when the streets shrank so, we couldn't move forward or turn. Poor Ricardo would have to back up agonizingly until we were back where we had started.

Despite all these problems, we had one only accident that could be described as serious. It happened during a long trip in Spain, from San Sebastian to Barcelona, when Stan Pelcher was driving. I can't remember what caused it, but all of a sudden we were crashing through a large plowed field and came to a stop at a crazy tilting angle. It took a long time and $100 to get a tow truck way out there, but what really upset me about the accident was that it broke up a bridge game I was winning. In fact, after we made sure there were no broken bones among us and that the tow truck was on its way, we went back to the game out there in the field. I won $12 while we were waiting.

The tour almost came to an abrupt end when, dead tired, we drove into a small town and, rather than get into a long involved conversation in a foreign language, I just motioned to the service-station attendant to fill up the tank. I didn't pay enough attention to observe that he was putting gasoline into our diesel engine. When we started to roll again, the bus nearly blew up.

On our first trip, we crossed over from Sweden into Denmark and piled out during the customs inspection. It was only when we reboarded a couple of hours later that we realized that Stan Pelcher was missing. He had gotten locked in the toilet in the back of the bus and nobody had heard him. Stan handled the whole thing very well. Instead of panicking, he just went to sleep. After that experience, I always counted bodies when we got off the bus.

It was no thing of beauty when we acquired it and with the wear we were giving it, the bus soon became one of Europe's great eyesores. There were bumps and scratches and scars all over and before long there were graffiti scrawled on every surface. All sorts of slogans were contributed by admiring hitchhikers and local townspeople. A New York subway rider would have felt right at home.

But as we drove throughout Europe—from north of the Arctic Circle to as far south as Gibraltar and as far east as Yugoslavia— we began to get attached to the crumbling old thing. If we were late getting to a game, the bus was big enough to dress in, and there were some nights out on the European highways when we simply pulled to the side of the road and slept in it. You can't spend ten months and 30,000 miles in a vehicle, I suppose, and not get sentimental about it.

Before we had the bus, the players always referred to our travels as The Tour. Afterwards, The Tour became The Bus. Even years later, long after it had gone into the retirement it so richly deserved, players from that era would ask, "Can I get back on The Bus?" when they wanted to know if I could find them a spot on the team.

It came as a shock to us when we finally lost the bus. In our last days riding it, we knew there was a lot wrong. The brakes were almost shot, the usable number of gears was down to about two and Ricardo Duarte had the strongest forearms in Western Europe from steering it. But we were still unprepared for the fact that there was a compulsory inspection for all Swedish vehicles when they returned to that country. I think the bus flunked on all counts.

I could have had it repaired, but it would have cost more than I had paid for it in the first place. In the end, we just left the bus parked outside of the basketball hall in Hälsingborg. When we came back the next year, it was gone. I didn't have the heart to ask what had happened to it.

Through all the years of the tour, I've aways tried to follow the motto of the post office. Neither rain nor sleet nor snow, etc. I will make every effort to get to a scheduled game. Every year, several teams announce tours and schedule games, but then don't show up for one reason or another. I've always wanted the reputation of honoring my commitments, figuring this principle would pay off in the long run. So in my time, I have chartered planes and hired cars when regular transportation fell through. I even hitched a ride on a yacht to get from one Italian resort city to another when there was a general strike.

Getting where you want to be on time often means leaving where you are in a hurry. So, like all coaches, I have my own tactics for the final moments of a game. Some coaches watch the clock in order to call a last-minute play that might win the game. I watch it to make sure we don't miss the train. Some coaches save their time-outs for late in the game, but I never use them. Some coaches have specialists for stalls late in the game, but I have five players charged with not stopping the clock, a couple getting into their clothes in the dressing room, another two or three changing on the bench and one guy out looking for a cab.

Nobody can get off the bench after a game faster than I can. I head right for the guy with the check, for whom I have usually begun to look with ten minutes to go. Some coaches head for the locker room. I go right to the ticket office.

Nevertheless, for all my planning and good intentions, Murphy's Law is operable at all times. Whatever can go wrong will go wrong. Always.

Take the times we've wound up in the wrong town. This isn't nearly as hard to accomplish as it might sound. The games are often scheduled only a few weeks in advance and, though my secretary in Trieste, Eva Bidovic, is extremely efficient, she has to chase me around Europe by phone. Very often something gets lost in the translation when she does find me.

Which is how one night, when 4,000 people were waiting for us in Clermont-Ferrand, France, I got us to a nice dark gym in Saint-Étienne, sixty miles away. I not only had to pay for all the expenses incurred in Clermont-Ferrand, I also had to give them a free game the following year.

The same thing happened in Yugoslavia, when we had a game scheduled in Brod. Ken Grant was handling the team, which arrived at the gym to find a bunch of kids out on the floor.

"Hey, want to play?" one of them shouted.

"Sure, that's what we're here for."

So they started playing a pick-up game when all of a sudden it hit Ken.

"Where's the crowd?" he said.

"You kidding?" one of the kids answered.

They learned they were not in Brod, but in Bosanski Brod, which was not far away. At least that time, they got where they were supposed to be in time to play the game.

There was once, though, when I *wanted* to be in two places at a time, and that caused headaches, too. Gillette, then our sponsor, arranged a special game in Paris that many of the company's French affiliates were to attend. After it had been set up, we were invited to play a game in London that the BBC was going to televise nationwide. We were to earn no extra fees, but I always go out of my way to play televised games, the best way of calling attention to the team.

Splitting up the team was no problem—we had done that often in the past—but the kicker was that *I* had to be in both places. Gillette wanted me at a pre-game reception and to be on the bench during the game, while the English federation considered it inconceivable for a team to play under its auspices without its coach on hand.

Even allowing for the fact that the starting times were more than an hour apart, I didn't see how I could be in both places at once. But I certainly didn't intend to disappoint either Gillette or the BBC. Finally, I worked out a solution. I attended the pregame reception in Paris, hung around for twelve or fourteen minutes of the first half of the game and then just took off, hoping nobody would miss me. I jumped into a cab, flew to London and made a mad dash to the arena there. I had nothing to worry about, as it turned out. I got there a full fifteen seconds before they went on the air. We won both games, too.

Then there was the time I lost the team completely, halfway around the world.

In 1970, we got a nice guarantee for a few games in Manila, to be followed by a tour of Australia. I put Ken Grant in charge and bid the players bon voyage. A week or so later in Rome, my telephone rang at three in the morning.

"Coach McGregor, this is Joe Sykes in Australia. Where's your team?"

"God, it's the middle of the night. Wait till I check my schedule—here, the team arrives on Qantas Flight 207 in Sydney at two o'clock this afternoon."

"I've got news for you. I'm at the Sydney airport and the flight's right in front of me and there isn't any basketball team on it."

"Christ! Give me your phone number. I'll find out what happened and call you back."

I called the hotel in Manila and was told the team had checked out many hours before. I called the Qantas manager in Rome, who was less than thrilled about being awakened at that hour.

"I put a basketball team on your plane," I said, "and it disappeared in midair."

"What kind of a nut are you?" he yawned.

"I may be a nut, but I'm trying to find fifteen people I booked on your Flight 207 from Manila to Sydney and I can't wait around."

"If I ever catch up with you, I'm going to give you a punch in the nose, but I'll check it out on the Telex."

A few minutes later, he called back.

"Flight 207 left Hong Kong, but due to a typhoon it couldn't land and had to overfly Manila and continue on to Australia."

"Well, let's get them on the next flight."

"We only fly once a week to Manila."

"Oh, Jesus. What rights do I have? Can I get a flight back to Hong Kong and another flight to Australia at your expense?"

"Under international air agreements, this is an act of God. We're not responsible because we couldn't land on account of the weather."

I called Australia and filled in Joe Sykes. "Hold on," I said. "I'll get back to you."

I was about to call the American Embassy and enlist its aid in the search for the team, when Ken Grant called. He had been trying to get through for hours.

"Can you figure out some way to get there?" I asked him.

"Not without flying back to Hong Kong."

Defeat. The upshot was, we went to Australia to earn $5,000 and ended up spending $10,000—a great way to do business.

Another time we were in Barcelona, Spain and scheduled to play in La Caruña. Franco was on vacation there, it was a big game, everything was set and—bang!—there was an airline strike at the last minute. We raced out to the airport, rounded up two small private planes and stuffed six bodies, ranging up to six feet ten in height, into each. It was a short trip, but a windy one. We never stopped bouncing—or throwing up. We got to the gym, covered with vomit, fifteen minutes before game time and the promoters were mad as hell because we were so late. But that's the reason people schedule us. They know we'll get there. It may cost us more than we're making, and we may not smell very nice, but we'll get there.

While travelling in Europe, a constant hazard is the general strike. All my split-second scheduling goes out the window when the workers of the world unite to shut down an entire country. In 1977, there were two strikes in France that tested my ingenuity to the utmost. Late in April, we had to go from Roanne to Mulhouse, a distance of about 240 miles, and the next day down to the French Riviera, about 550 miles. To get to Mulhouse, we went by way of Switzerland, which was not the shortest route, but, due to the strike, the cheapest. A rented bus got us out of France to Geneva, a Swiss train took us to Basel and from there we rented a second bus to Mulhouse. Cost of renting the two buses —$500. Income from the game in Mulhouse—$500.

That leg of the trip was a joy compared with getting to the Riviera. A Swiss train got us through that country and we transferred to an Italian train that took us to Genoa. But avalanches, caused by heavy rains, had interrupted rail service along the Riviera, so we had to use buses to get back to the French border. There, we encountered the strike again and had to rent cars to make the game. Still, not all of us made it. Curt Peterson, a seven-footer, had not been comfortable in the Italian sleeping car and had moved into the next coach during the night. Early in the morning, his car was switched off into the Milan railroad yard and there he awoke while we were on our way to Genoa.

Three weeks later, there was another general strike which forced me to do what I hate most—cancel games. We had three games scheduled in Barcelona, after which we were to take a night sleeper to a tournament in Le Mans and then continue on to Italy. Unable to rely on the trains, part of this schedule had to be abandoned and, since we expected to make more money at Le Mans than Barcelona, I cancelled out in Spain. A mistake. Le Mans postponed its tournament for a day because of the strike, so we could have gone to Spain after all. In addition, we were out of the tournament in Italy, with a loss of $1,500 in income and five extra days of idleness as the net result.

I only wish that had been the end of the story. Four new players were flying via charter from the United States to Zurich and I had told them to join us in Barcelona. But our last-minute change of plans meant we weren't going to be in Barcelona. How could I tell them to join us in France? It's all but impossible to reach passengers on a chartered plane when it lands. The charter lines generally have no staff at the airports to take messages and the scheduled airlines hate the low-cost charters so much they aren't about to help.

So I had to pull out all the stops. I called the U.S. Consulate in Zurich, the airport police there and the information bureau at the airport. I even called the presidents of basketball clubs in Zurich—men I didn't know—and asked them for help. One of these methods worked because the players arrived at the Hotel Ambassador in Paris, as instructed. The trouble is, they got there before we did—I had assumed they would spend the night in Zurich—and found all the rooms full and no message from me. This cheered them up considerably after their long trip.

There was one—and only one—occasion when not being able to play a game was not a disaster. In 1954, shortly before I went to Italy for the first time, I wangled an invitation for the Portland State basketball team to play in Saigon, enabling me to write a nice chunk of business for the airline I represented. We had been guaranteed $1,000 for each of two games, but we got to Saigon just ahead of a typhoon, which washed out the games.

I was sitting in the hotel feeling sorry for myself, when a member of the local Chinese community, which had promoted the games, showed up and said how unhappy he was that the games had been cancelled. He had passed the hat, he said, to make up our losses. He turned over exactly $2,000. I was so grateful that the following year we came back and played an extra game for nothing.

Often, the inconveniences we encounter on the tour are more

comic than desperate. Once, we were playing in Stockholm and I got us berths in a sleeper going to the north of Sweden for our next game. The extra expense was worth it because we were saving the cost of hotel rooms. I made sure that we got to the station two hours ahead of time and that all our luggage was ready to load, but I wasn't prepared for the distractions we ran into. They were mostly blonde, all beautiful and there were enough to go around. Even I had somebody to talk to. We were buying them Cokes and sandwiches and having a delightful time when we all seemed to realize at once that our train had left fifteen minutes earlier.

It was the last train of the night and the first train the next day wouldn't get us up north in time for our game there. On top of that, there was no scheduled airline service. Not only did I have to play the role of millionaire hunter and charter a plane, I also had to get us hotel rooms in Stockholm. Luckily, four or five of the players didn't need hotel rooms that night. They had done well enough at the train station.

Another time, in 1977, we were travelling through France during a holiday weekend and arrived at the station to find the entire train sold out. Undaunted, I requisitioned the baggage car, which got us where we were going but only at the cost of an unmerciful ribbing from the players about this second-class treatment.

A few weeks later, though, we took a train ride that drew no complaints. From Zagreb to Belgrade, we shared a sleeping car with twenty vacationing Danish nurses. For the next four days, in fact, we had twenty cheerleaders on tour with us. They got bigger hands from the crowd than we did and, as our performances lagged, our morale rose. When they finally went home, along went two players, who resigned abruptly from the team.

In the years of the tour, we have gone to Eastern Europe regularly, and, while there's never been any trouble once we arrived, the travelling can cause more than its share of problems. Just setting up the tour can take forever. First, the basketball federation of the country in question must get permission from the government to invite us. Then the federation invites us. Then it goes back to the government to get permission to issue visas. Then a Telex is sent to its embassy in whatever country we are in, telling us to pick up the visas. You don't just hop on a plane and go.

As for the travelling itself, I have often counted myself lucky that I am not breaking up rocks in some nice Eastern European quarry as a result of some of our adventures. I once took my Levi's team from Vienna to Prague in an overnight sleeping car. This is a fairly short trip, less than 200 miles, but during it we were awakened at least ten times by officials who wanted to inspect our passports and our luggage. To make things worse, there was a special officer for customs, a special officer for passports and a railway policeman. The line outside the door seemed to get longer and longer. These were my hippie players, who were not exactly awed by authority and they soon got the impression that the various officials were most interested in checking up, not on us, but on each other.

"Watch out," one of the players would say to one cop, "he looks like a spy to me."

"Don't let him get away with that," somebody else would say to another, and so on.

Luckily, the police didn't speak English, or we might still be there.

My hairiest experience travelling in Eastern Europe took place on one cold night in 1968. We had a game scheduled in West Berlin and the East German police decided to search every car on the autobahn. We were running late when we pulled up and stopped behind what looked like forty miles of waiting cars. What to do?

A bribe was out of the question; that could bring a long-term coaching contract in prison. The bus hardly looked like an ambulance or a vehicle that could claim diplomatic immunity. Nevertheless, I decided to pull out of line and drive past all those waiting cars. At first, the police seemed too surprised to react, but at the next roadblock we were greeted by enough red lights and sirens to make us homesick for American television. I stared a policeman in the face and appealed to the German god of promptness.

"We will be late for an important basketball game in East Berlin," I said. I pulled out our contract and waved it in his face, hoping he wouldn't look at it long enough to see that it said, very clearly, that the game was to be played in *West* Berlin. It seemed to work. The policeman waved us past the miles of waiting cars, and escorted us as well. I was congratulating myself on my triumph when we crossed the checkpoint entrance to the city and he pulled us over.

"McGregor," he said, "you are lucky it was me. I am a basketball coach, too, and remember you from the Italian national team."

After we arrived, the game was delayed. It was to be played on a military base and, after months without seeing a hamburger, a trip to the PX was the first order of business. The players warmed up with a burger in each hand, sipping milkshakes as they passed the bench.

The next night, we played in a big German sports hall against a team of Turks who were working in Berlin. I had coached many of the Turkish players and, were it not for the fact that the scoreboard and the toilets worked, I might have thought I was back in Istanbul.

Finally, though, we left East Germany, which is more than the East Germans can do.

Making sure we have all our luggage and equipment with us is another constant problem. I have sent players into games with borrowed shoes, old T-shirts and even in jeans. There are also jock-strap forgetters, but generally this doesn't happen more than once per player, since nobody ever seems willing to lend one and the forgetter has to play, anyhow.

Once, we got to the train station early and, as usual, we piled all our luggage together on the platform. One of the players went off somewhere, asking another to watch his stuff. Apparently, he misjudged the time of departure because we were just beginning to roll when he ran up and jumped on the train.

"Did you watch my stuff?" he asked the other player.

"Yeah, I'm still watching it. It's right out there."

And he pointed to the platform where his buddy's luggage was receding into the distance.

Then there's the question of what to do with the gifts and awards that come our way during the tour. Just about every tournament presents a trophy or a present to all the participants and, since travelling light is the key to survival, this can make for difficulty if the gift is big or heavy.

Most of the tournaments are sponsored by local companies and the gifts are often their products. If a wine company is the host, it's traditional to present a bottle to each player before the game. Nobody wants to carry bottles around, so sometimes the reddish tint in the water we're drinking on the bench isn't the result of local mineral deposits. Wine before meals may be all right, but during time-outs?

It's harder to dispose of some other gifts. Once we played in a tournament sponsored by a manufacturer of ladies' lingerie and this was a great test of our ingenuity. It's easy to give away whiskey or cigarettes, but what do you do with a selection of brassieres?

In 1977, in a tournament in Bari, Italy, Paul Coder, an excellent big man from North Carolina State, was named most valuable player. For this, he won two rolls of wallpaper. In Israel once, we were given oranges and instructions on what to do in an air raid. Sometimes, the gifts are very warmly received, indeed. It was certainly hard to beat Kuwait's choice of Rolex watches all around. And in Denmark, pretty girls gave us all flowers before a game. I don't know what became of the flowers, but we saw a lot of the girls during our stay there.

After twenty-five years of living and coaching in Europe, I have amassed hundreds of trophies, some of them very beautiful. At one time, it might have been feasible to ship them home, but the cost now would exceed the combined real and sentimental value. Unless I can get a steamship company to sponsor a tour soon, I'll have to find a way to dispose of them. I'm toying with the idea of giving them back to the clubs that awarded them in the first place. They can institute the Jim McGregor Trophy for the player who spends the most time on the bench.

There are two more problems that face the itinerant basketball traveller in Europe. One involves the biggest gap between U.S. and foreign facilities—the locker room. This may go back to the concept that athletes should be hardy Spartans who can put up with anything, but American players are unprepared for what they find in Europe. Years ago, my coaches would threaten to send players to the locker room for a breach of discipline. There are places in Europe where I wouldn't do that for anything short of a felony.

The stench is the first thing you notice. The toilets are often open and seldom very clean. The toilet paper is that rough brown substance that is such a favorite in much of the world—when it's there at all. Many American travellers carry rolls of money with them. My players often carry rolls of toilet paper.

As for the facilities themselves, there is sometimes little more than a cold park bench and a hook. Hangers are a definite luxury. Often the locker rooms are so small and crowded together that we can hear the other team talking next door, which detracts somewhat from pregame and halftime strategy sessions. And, in many of the outdoor stadiums we've played, the locker rooms are security areas where you retreat to hide from angry mobs. These have no windows, so the fans can't throw anything in at you. Thus they are little more than sealed vaults beneath the stadiums.

We have used locker rooms in churches that were really old wine cellars, and the players were far more interested in looking for a leftover bottle than in listening to me. In Africa, where we often played outdoors, there were generally no locker rooms at all. At halftime, we would just leave the court and sit in the grass and chat. Lately, with the new arenas that are being built all over Europe, this locker-room gap is being closed somewhat. We don't change in the hotel as often in order to reduce the amount of time spent in the locker room.

Last, but not least, there's the constant battle I fight with European telephones.

In France, I have to leave my nice suite at the Hotel Ambassador, go across the street and stand in line at the post office to use the telephone. The hotel doubles the charge to place the call and I think it has invented the fifty-second minute; by the time everything is added up, the bill is about four times what it should be. The hotel even charges five dollars to make a collect call.

At the post office, I earn every penny I save. Calls are placed through an operator who, like every other French civil servant I have dealt with, gives the impression that her work is interrupting something she would much rather be doing. There are some coin phones that can be used to bypass the post-office operator, but the odds are better on a Las Vegas slot machine.

At night, I often take a cab to the central post office, where there are direct-dial booths. But the line is often busy when you pick up the telephone, a phenomenon that has reduced me to a raving maniac on more than one occasion. Or, if you do get through, the chances are good that you will be cut off. Also, you have to wait in line to get a booth, wait in line again to pay and, finally, wait in the middle of the night for a taxi.

Still, I can't do business without the telephone, which leaves me wide open for conversations like the one I had in 1977, with a Mr. Wao in Taiwan. I was lining up some European players for a tournament there and he sent me a telegram asking me to call him. Naturally, I assumed he spoke English or some European language. Bad assumption.

McGregor (shouting over the static of a bad line): Wao?
Wao (shouting back): Wao!
McGregor: Wao?
Wao: Wao!
McGregor: Wao, this is McGregor.
Wao: McGregor? Wao. Wao.
McGregor: Wao, speak English.
Wao: No speak English.
McGregor: Wow, what a mess.
Wao: Wao.
Operator: That will be eighty-five dollars for three minutes.
McGregor and Wao: WAO!

CHAPTER **20**

Black and Blue and Pink

THERE ARE TIMES when the tour resembles a 1930s dance marathon in which the tempo never slackens. We have played twenty-two games in twenty-three nights, with long days of travel in between. Yet the players seem to prosper through it all, and years later we will run into each other and recall the hard times like soldiers at a reunion remembering battles fought together.

It is the rare breaks and layoffs, in fact, that seem to make us let down. I usually arrange a week on the French Riviera after a long stretch of travelling as a way of getting a little rest and having some fun. We still play every night, but the days are given over to the nude beaches. It's easy to tell which players have visited them because the tender pink of their skin doesn't mix well with the black and blue of roughhouse basketball. For the first few days after arriving at the Riviera, the game is played the way it was intended—as a non-contact sport.

I used to think we would resume our travels with renewed vigor after such a stop, but it doesn't always work out that way. Very often, some of the players never seem to get back to playing their best and sometimes they disappear from the tour. After seeing one hundred miles of bare breasts, maybe they figure there's nothing left in the world for them to experience and they might as well return to Philadelphia.

A prime attraction of the tour is the Italian summer tournament season, a unique combination of tourist attraction, civic festival and basketball. The tournaments are held at resort cities along the coast and financed by municipal funds. The finals are usually televised on Wednesday nights and watching them has become something of a tradition, like Monday-night football in the United States. Very often, a city will receive more national publicity through its tournament than it will get the rest of the year.

There's never a shortage of spectators. A town like Rimini, for instance, will swell from its normal population of 60,000 or 70,000 during the off-season to over a million during the summer because of its extremely long beach filled with apartment houses, hotels and *pensiones*. When the tournament is played there, the arena is always full.

At first, the tournaments only involved Italian teams, but as the matches became more popular, officials would bring in a few outsiders to ensure good performances. Finally, they began inviting entire foreign teams. In the early 1960s, the tournaments became truly international. There was always a strong Yugoslavian team and very often a team from the Soviet Union and Brazil. In fact, some countries—Russia, in particular—took to sending their national teams to benefit from the strong competition. Tradition frowned on national teams competing as such in unofficial tournaments because many player-eligibility rules were not enforced, but it was easy to get around this by simply giving the team a new name. The Russians usually entered as the Moscow All-Stars or the Soviet Army, but the players were almost all members of the national team.

For the last decade or so, my touring team has been the North American representative in the Italian summer tournaments and we seldom fail to have a good time. Italy leads the world in vacations the way Sweden is tops in cashed-in return tickets. We go from one coast to another, from north to south, visiting all the lovely resort cities—Venice, Chieti, Rapallo, Ischia and others—

meeting vacationers from all over the world. We stay in each city for three or four days. The games are played as doubleheaders that don't start until 9 P.M. or end until after midnight. After that, we have a fashionably late dinner, repair to a bar or discotheque and get to bed quite late. We sleep until noon at least and then enjoy a few hours on the beach and a nap before the game.

There have been tournaments in as many as seventeen cities, although a few have dropped out recently because of the Italian recession and the devaluation of the lira, which makes it hard to pay the foreign teams the guarantees they ask.

In the Italian summer tournaments in the last decade, we played the Soviet Union six times and won twice, which was quite an accomplishment since Russia was using her best players. All the games we played against the Russians were very close. We also seemed to be at our best against Yugoslavia, which always had one of the best teams in the world. The Yugoslavs liked to play our game—running and wide open—unlike the Soviets, whose patient, tactical methods usually didn't suit our mood or temperament after a hard day at the beach.

One of the most interesting tournaments of the Italian summer season takes place in Siena, where the neighborhood bars all sponsor teams. Undoubtedly, the tradition began with the patrons and employees of the bar playing each other, but it has gone way beyond that now. One bar probably found an outsider who was a good player, then another one used two ringers and so on. At any rate, in Siena now the best club players in Italy and a lot of top foreigners compete under the auspices of Joe's Bar or Tony's Bar. In fact, I get $2,500 to send my players down and the bars divide them up, using two or three on each team. The players love it because they earn more playing for Joe or Tony than they do playing for me. Also, the post-game celebrations are on the house. Siena recently built a new arena that holds about 10,000 spectators and games are sold out for three or four straight nights during the tournament.

The change in routine, from the tightly scheduled tour to the late hours we keep during the Italian summer-tournament season, can sometimes be a lot to handle for players who have gotten used to the boredom of constant travelling. One night in Luano, in 1969, one of the players, John Schetzele from Ashland College, got into serious trouble.

After more than one convivial round in a waterfront bar, John decided to take a run down the beach and ran smack into the prow of a fishing boat that had been pulled up onto the sand. John was so anesthetized by liquor that he didn't feel much pain. Amazingly, he was able to make his way back to the hotel and go to sleep.

The next morning, the player rooming with him woke up to loud strangling sounds. He looked over to find the other bed drenched with blood and John unable to speak. He shouted for help. Several of us came running. We bandaged John's head cut and rushed him to the hospital. Except for the cut, the doctors couldn't find any signs of injury severe enough to have affected his speech. As we were trying to figure out what was wrong, John asked for a piece of paper and wrote out, "Running on beach—something hit head."

The hospital brought in a brain surgeon who found a deep puncture wound, much more severe than it first appeared. As he examined the injury, he said, "This is very, very dangerous. Not only has the blow damaged his ability to speak, but it has pushed hair into the brain. Hair is a great carrier of disease. I'll have to operate at once."

Luckily, he turned out to be a fine surgeon. After he opened the skull and cleaned out the wound, John's speech began to return immediately. It kept improving and within a few days, it was normal. However, the doctor was still quite concerned about him.

"Now, son, you've got to be very careful," he said. "You can't take another blow on the head like that. You've got to avoid contact sports and live a quiet life."

John, who was still scared to death, said, "Oh, don't worry about it. My athletic career is over."

He remained in the hospital for four months before returning home. A year later, he was trying out with San Diego of the ABA.

Most of the time, my touring teams play for a set fee guaranteed by the host club or tournament or, in the case of a big event, for a share of the profits. The sponsoring body generally expects to recover its costs from gate receipts and, perhaps, television revenue. There have been times, however, when we have been invited to put on what amounts to basketball exhibitions. In countries where the game hasn't been widely developed we are brought in as a sort of inspiration to the national team and to show how basketball looks when it's well played.

In 1967, my Gulf team made a trip of this sort to Kuwait. We flew there from Tehran and, between the time we took off and the time we landed, the six-day Arab-Israeli war broke out. As the representatives of an American oil company, we were a little nervous, but the Kuwaiti officials seemed determined to treat us correctly. The only reminder of what was going on came from a group of kids who were standing a distance away, shouting and gesturing. They managed to sail one or two rocks into our midst, but otherwise there were no incidents during our stay, which lasted longer than the war did.

There were six or seven sports clubs in Kuwait, but all the players seemed to come from other countries. There were Egyptians, Greeks, Lebanese and so forth—all working in Kuwait at the time. The local people seemed interested only in owning and running the club teams.

We had little difficulty defeating Kuwait's national team, such as it was, and, when the game was over, federation officials asked if we would divide up our own squad into two groups and give a demonstration. I hesitated. Though we had ten players, one of them had a sore ankle. Then some of the players started needling me. "Come on, coach. Show them what you can do." So I agreed to be the tenth man.

Before the game started, I called a team meeting and outlined the ground rules. I was in fairly decent shape, but I was twenty years older and a foot shorter than most of the players. I could stand a zone defense or a man-to-man, I said, but under no circumstances was I to be pressed all over the court. I didn't want one of those healthy young cats embarrassing me by stealing the ball.

So there in Kuwait, before an audience of Arabs in white robes (no women, of course), I played my last competitive basketball game. Some of the people in the crowd must have wondered why that short old bald guy was getting the ball all the time. It was because I was the coach and when the coach says, "Give me the damn ball," he gets it.

I played what I guess you could call a tactical game, very close to the mid-court line. I didn't get back very far on defense and I got off a little early when my side had the ball. With the cooperation of the players, this meant I was able to receive some passes that went for fast-break layups and could do a fair amount of dribbling.

I thought it went pretty well, actually, although I kept intact my record of fifteen years without a rebound. But the next day, the players kidded me unmercifully about the fact that I hadn't moved around very much. A couple of them started pantomiming my movements—or rather lack of them—on the court and pretty soon everybody was doubled over in laughter, myself included.

We were at the Gulf compound in Kuwait at the time and it had a swimming pool. So after I took this abuse for a while, I said casually, "I'll tell you what. I'll bet anybody here that I can beat him in ten laps of the pool."

I'm sure that with any practice they all could have beaten me. But none of them had been doing any real swimming, while I have always tried to get in a mile a day whenever possible since I first won some swimming championships in high school. I thought the odds would be on my side.

Four or five of the players took the challenge and the betting got pretty interesting. I think there might have been $200 or $300 at stake. The pool was an odd length—33⅓ yards, as I recall —and when the race started, the boys all sprinted way out ahead of me. Since they hadn't been practicing and didn't know how to pace themselves, I was content to bide my time and play tortoise to their hares.

Sure enough, I was behind all of them at 100 yards and some of them at 200 yards, but, by the time we turned for the final lap, several of the players had dropped out exhausted. I beat those who were left by a couple of body lengths. There was a little more respect for the old man after that. It helped ease the sting of my retirement as a basketball player, too.

CHAPTER **21**

"Let's Get Out of Here Alive"

A GREAT DEAL is said about the use of sport as a political tool and there is no question that you can tell a lot about a country's economic and social philosophies from the way its athletic programs are handled. The establishment of huge training centers in East Germany to produce championship athletes for the greater glory of communism reflects the way that country sees the world, just as professional ballplayers signing $3-million contracts tells volumes about the United States.

Usually, these discussions portray the politics of sports as nothing more than a clash of ideologies. This is a mistake, I believe. There is far more involved, much of it quite positive.

Long before the Soviet Union established diplomatic relations with many non-communist countries, it began a quest for sports ties. Looking back, it is possible to see that it was through its athletes that Russia began emerging from post-World War II isolation. In 1950, the Soviets participated in the world basketball championships in Chile, despite the fact that they had no political or commercial relationships with that country. The first Soviet contacts with much of Latin America came through sports.

The most amazing demonstration I have ever witnessed of the power of sport as a positive political tool took place in 1954, at the first Asian Games in Manila. The Philippines had been anxious to host the games, but there had been great concern about how the Japanese team would be received. Japan had occupied the Philippines during the war and had instituted a reign of terror. Nearly everybody in Manila had felt its wrath, either personally or through a friend or relative who had been imprisoned, tortured or killed. There was no great desire to see the Japanese return any time soon.

But once the decision was made to host the games, the government undertook a massive public-relations campaign. This is a great opportunity, the Filipinos were told. We must make the most of it. We must not look back. The Japanese are our guests. Still, nobody knew how it would work out and there was quite a bit of apprehension.

The stadium where the games were held had been used by the Japanese during the war as a mass concentration camp. Some of the people in the stands that day undoubtedly had been prisoners there only ten years earlier. Protocol at international meets calls for the raising of the victorious country's flag and the playing of its anthem after each event. Since Japan was the dominant athletic power in Asia then, the Rising Sun and the Japanese anthem were seen and heard again and again. Yet each time, the Filipinos rose and stood quietly. There wasn't a single incident or protest, though I'm sure the war could not have been far from anybody's mind.

I have, however, witnessed political demonstrations at sports events. In fact, I've been in the middle of more than a few.

In 1967, the second year my team was sponsored by Gulf, we went to Latin America on what was basically a successful, enjoyable tour. But it also included the single most frightening game in which I have ever been involved. It happened in Panama, where the style of basketball was rough to begin with. Basketball was not a largely middle- or upper-class game in Panama, as it was in much of Latin America. It was played primarily by poor blacks who had developed a style that made the pushing and shoving in the NBA seem tame by comparison.

The fans reacted in kind. Recently, a new arena has been built in Panama City and the seats are set back from the floor a little. But on this trip, we played in a national-guard armory in the toughest part of town, where the fans sat right up by the court.

It was just our luck that, at the time of our visit, anti-American feelings were running high. The Panama Canal issue, never far beneath the surface, was red-hot; a sniper had just fired on the U.S. army barracks and a military alert had been called. In we came, representing the great imperialist oil company. A number of Panamanians in the armory carried knives and we could sense the hostility all around us. I believe I gave one of my shortest and most memorable pre-game talks:

"Now, boys, let's get out of here alive."

The situation got out of hand almost from the beginning. For one thing, the Panamanian team was almost as good as it was rough. It played very solid, rugged basketball. For another, it was clear that the referees, two members of the local Chinese community, were scared to death. They were both prominent businessmen in Panama and neither one had the slightest intention of antagonizing the local players or fans. As soon as the game began, I saw that we were going to set a record not only for fouls, but also for travelling, three-second violations and anything else the referees could think of.

Despite this, and despite the fact that we were constantly being grabbed, held, shoved and knocked around, we played a sensational game of basketball. In all my years of coaching, I never had a team play so well or so luckily. Everything we did came out right. In the first half, we must have shot eighty percent and we completely dominated the backboards. At one point, Bill Bradley—a fine little guard from Tennessee State, not the former Princeton and New York Knick star—passed the ball to Rich Nieman, our center from St. Louis University. Just as Rich was about to reach for the ball, two Panama players grabbed his arms from behind and pulled him down. The ball bounced off Rich's chest right into the hands of one of our players under the basket and he scored easily. That kind of thing happened all night.

When we left the court at halftime, the game was tied. In the locker room, I reminded everybody that, as nice as it would be to win the game, the top priority was to get out of there in one piece. When we came back after the intermission, it appeared that, once again, I had neglected my halftime defense. We now trailed by four points. When I mentioned this to the scorekeeper, he said, "Are you calling me a liar?" and strongly suggested I get back to the bench. Under the circumstances, it seemed like a good idea.

Actually, I had made a mistake arguing over the score. I should have used the time to outfit the team in shoulder pads and helmets because the second half was the roughest, dirtiest session of basketball I have ever seen. One of Panama's worst players—but best fighters—made it his personal mission to put Bradley out of the game. It was good strategy because, at five feet ten, Bill may have been the best player, inch for inch, who has ever played on one of my teams. And when Bill was challenged, he stood his ground and fought. One of the referees made his best move of the night by throwing out both players, thereby preventing a riot and saving Bill's life.

Shortly after this, another Panama player took a punch at John Lescher, a big forward, who put up a hand to block it. The result was a broken wrist. Now we were without two of our best players. Still, we kept playing this amazing game of basketball, hanging onto a small lead. One of the reasons was Al Dillard, a big tough forward who played at American University after a stint in the Marine Corps. Nobody knew how old Al was; he was something of a Satchel Paige of basketball because he had been around so long. Apparently, he enjoyed his return to hand-to-hand combat. There seemed to be a neutral zone around Al where the Panamanian players kept going down as he hammered them to the floor. But Al would just pick them up and go on getting the rebounds and blocking the shots.

Not everybody was as anxious to mix it up as Al was. Dick Smith, a forward from Seattle, was happy to hang around mid-court where he had an unobstructed view of the exits at both ends of the floor. He even fired a couple of shots from that area and they went in, too. The game stayed very close and, against my better judgment and instinct for survival, I began to root hard for us to win.

After one bad call, I ran out onto the court and yelled, "You yellow son of a bitch!" at the Chinese referee before I realized what I was doing. By then, both officials were stationed under the baskets, which was as close to the exits as they could get and still be on the court.

By the end, we were down to four players. Everybody else had fouled out and the clock seemed to be going fast both ways—forward when we were behind and backward when we were ahead. Finally, Panama scored a basket, went ahead by a point and the buzzer sounded. It was hard getting to the locker room through a shower of everything in the building that wasn't nailed down, but it was even harder to get out. We stayed there for two hours before Panamanian troops finally escorted us back to our hotel.

The next day, the director of the Panamanian federation came by the hotel to say what a great game it had been and how much the crowd had loved it. Why didn't we stay for another? he asked.

"Only if it's sponsored by the Red Cross," I said, and for the first time in my life I turned down a good guarantee. We went off to Nicaragua where all we had to worry about was a volcano erupting. It did, but we hardly noticed.

Another game in which politics were intricately involved took place in the late 1960s in Ragusa, a town in southern Sicily, where Gulf wanted us to play because it had found a little oil nearby. It was like taking a trip back in time: an isolated village where everybody, men and women, still dressed in black and there were few modern buildings. Ragusa turned out to be one of the few cities in Italy where there was any real communist influence at the time—it has grown much stronger in recent years—and it even had a communist mayor. Our opponent in the game was the Soviet Union's national team, which had won the world championship the previous year, in one of its various disguises.

We had a clue to what was in store when we arrived. In the center of the town square was the biggest flag I have ever seen— the Hammer and Sickle. All around it were smaller Russian flags.

Lost in there somewhere was one American flag, about six inches by four inches. At the reception, everybody had a red banner and the mayor gave a long florid speech that was translated into Russian. Then the Russian coach stood up and made a long speech in return that was translated into Italian.

This took the better part of an hour. When it was over, the Russian coach brought out a huge box and gave it to the mayor. Inside, was a selection of eight different types of Russian vodka and the mayor embraced him. For a moment, I thought he was going to cry in gratitude. The mayor then presented the Russian coach with a huge silver platter and there were more hugs and emotional words of thanks. I expected the strains of "The Internationale" to break out at any moment.

Then it was our turn. I walked up, said I was glad to be there and gave the mayor our usual gift, a Gulf pennant. Wholesale price—five cents. He said welcome to Ragusa, gave me a small trinket worth easily as much and the reception was over.

Before the game, I told the team that the Russians were good rough players, that it was all right to play hard and that I certainly wanted to win. But we weren't in the friendliest of territories so it might be just as well if we didn't start something we couldn't handle.

The moment I finished, Neil Johnson, our big strong center, said, "I'm going to kill those Commie bastards."

On the first play of the game, the Russian center went in for a layup and Neil creamed him. That set the stage for one of the greatest games of power basketball ever played. Physically, the Russians take second place to nobody, and my team got into the spirit of it right away. The game was extremely hard-fought, with players landing elbows and bumping heads and pushing each other down on the floor from start to finish. The referees did the wisest thing they could have done under the circumstances— nothing. They didn't call fouls on either team, so it worked out just fine.

Toward the end, there was a time-out and my players came off the floor. Neil Johnson, all battered and bruised, looked at me through one half-closed eye and another with a cut over it and said, "These guys aren't so bad." That was the ultimate compliment to the world champions. We won the game by a couple of points.

Later that night, both teams ended up in the only movie theater in town. Neither side could understand the Italian—although there were enough guns and breasts on the screen so that the dialogue wasn't that important and they spent most of their time laughing about the game, exchanging pins and so on. After knocking heads a few times, they really got along quite well.

Perhaps the most emotional fan demonstration I ever saw was prompted by international politics. It happened in 1968 during the Italian summer tournaments in which a team from Czechoslovakia was entered. No sooner had the tournaments begun than a revolution in Czechoslovakia broke out and the Russians counterattacked. It was a terrible time for the Czech players, who knew nothing about what was happening to their families and friends. They had no communication with anyone inside their country and were in agony as they heard continuing reports about the fighting and the bloodshed. We were with them every day, sharing their suspense and helplessness. The response in Italy was extremely volatile and even the Italian communists denounced the Russian invasion. It was a tremendously emotional time for all of us.

When we got to the town of Roseto, the fighting seemed to be at its height and it was there that this fan demonstration took place. We were to play the Czechs in the first round of the tournament and when their team was introduced the crowd rose in a mass, shouting and cheering. The noise grew and grew with no sign of ever stopping. It went on like that—I swear it—for two solid hours. There was simply no way the crowd was going to allow that game to be played until it had drained itself of all the emotion and sympathy that was in it. The Czech players were overwhelmed; soon they and we and everybody in the arena were all weeping. Even today, I can't think of that moment without beginning to cry all over again.

No matter where we are playing, it's important to be aware of the local political situation. One year, I had a team in Manila during an election campaign when everybody seemed to be going around armed. It was a little nerve-racking to look up into the packed stands and see a holster under every armpit. A cleaner game of basketball never was played—at least on our side. I told the players that if they ran into anybody by mistake to be sure to grab him before he hit the floor. Whenever a foul was called, everybody on the team raised his hand. In fact, some of the players raised both hands.

The fellow who has to put up with the most politics, I would guess, is the coach of the national team of Lebanon. The country is split between the Moslems and the Christians, and government policy is that everything official—the army, the parliament and so on—must be divided evenly down the middle. Alas, nobody has yet figured out a way to divide five basketball players into two equal groups. Two Moslems, two Christians and an Armenian, perhaps.

In 1969, I took a Gulf team to Lebanon, and we played in an excellent arena along the Mediterranean, five or six miles south of Beirut. The game was nationally televised and the spectators were a divided group. The Christian community cheered for the Christians on the Lebanese team, the Moslems cheered for the Moslems and the Americans in the crowd cheered for us. I came away with the feeling there will never be unified fan support for the Lebanese team.

An inflamed political situation isn't always necessary for trouble to break out on the basketball court. Almost any incident or circumstance will do. It almost seems as if there is a tide to these things and, once it gets started, it simply has to be played out to the conclusion.

In 1976, I had a team in Ypres, a town in Belgium that is best remembered as the scene of a World War I battle where hundreds of thousands of soldiers were killed. I got the urge to commit a little mayhem myself while we were there.

It was strictly an exhibition game, of no real significance, except for a couple of extenuating circumstances. There was a new coach who was anxious to make a good showing, and Ypres was traditionally the most difficult place to play in Belgium. There were more incidents there every year than anywhere else in the country. One reason for this was that there was a beer parlor right in the stands. The fans didn't even have to get up and stand in line to order. They could just sit at a table and watch the game while signalling the waiter to bring them beer after beer.

The new coach wanted to use some of our players to see if they would fit in with his club and I agreed to lend him four of them for the game. When we got to the arena, however, I found we were scheduled to play a doubleheader. Since I had lent out four players, I was down to only eight. I had to tell several of them they would have to dress for both games. By the time the second game started, I was confused about which players I had told to be ready for which game and I forgot to enter one player's name in the official's book.

The game got pretty rough and the other coach, anxious to make a good first impression, was soon bobbing back and forth, giving me the finger and yelling unpleasant remarks in several languages at me and my players. During the second half, several of my players fouled out and I sent in the man whose name I had forgotten to register with the officials. The other coach went wild.

"You can't play him!" he shouted. "His name's not on the book!"

"Wait a minute!" I yelled back. "I'm down to four players now because I'm lending *you* players. It's only an exhibition game. Don't get so excited."

But he was adamant and we got into a pretty violent argument. This wasn't lost on the fans and they began to howl. One of them came running down from his seat in the beer garden and the next thing we knew one of my players, Rupert Breedlove, had beer down his neck and back. The fan had made an unwise choice. Rupert Breedlove was six feet ten, weighed 250 pounds and might have been the strongest man in Belgium at that moment. I wouldn't have gone near him with a drop of beer. Rupert showed admirable restraint, I thought, by merely turning around and pushing the cup of beer back into the fan's face.

But it provoked enough of a riot that the referees called the game and we shoved our way into the locker room. Shortly after we had gotten there, a bunch of police showed up.

"Where's Breedlove?" one demanded.

"Why?" I said.

"The guy he hit said he was dizzy and couldn't see," the cop said. "He's in the hospital."

By then, we had sneaked Rupert out to the team bus and, when the players heard my conversation with the police, a few of them drove him away. I told the police I would go to the hospital to see the injured party. Without the beer in his hand or blood system, he didn't seem quite so brave.

"Listen, I told him, "if Rupert Breedlove had hit you, your wife would be a widow and your children would be fatherless. Now, let's be realistic. Whatever happened, he didn't hit you with any force. He may have given you a push to keep you off his neck."

But it was no good. A warrant was issued, charging Rupert with assault and battery. Luckily, he was no longer around for it to be served on him. The other players had driven him the few miles it took to cross the French border. That's the advantage of playing in small countries. You can get out quickly.

Sometimes a player can get so wrapped up in the game that, without thinking, he can cause the worst kind of trouble. This happened once when Ralph Telken, who was as intense a player as I ever coached, was on a Gulf team. Ralph played at Rockhurst College in Kansas City and led his team to the national NAIA championship. Nobody played defense like Ralph and nobody was as dedicated. I am convinced he had no interests other than basketball—no mistress was ever more loved—and no use for anyone who didn't take it seriously. Even when we were playing a game every night, Ralph would go out in the morning and take a thousand shots. He worked hard at staying cool during games and he never blew up. Except once.

In 1967, we were playing in an important Italian summer-league tournament in Loano, and the Russian national team, disguised as a Moscow all-star squad, was also playing in it. If we both won our semifinal games, we would meet for the championship. Our game was against a weak Italian team from Milan and we were winning easily. But Ralph never let up for a minute on defense; he guarded his man perfectly all through the game. Finally, the frustrated Milan player couldn't take it any longer and he ran right over Ralph, really stomping on him.

The referee whistled a foul on Ralph, a terrible call, and Ralph was furious. A minute later, the same thing happened again and the referee made the same call. Ralph was absolutely boiling by then and I could see he wanted to kill somebody. I really should have taken him out of the game, but I figured it would be over soon and surely it couldn't happen again. Wrong. On the third bad call, Ralph decked the referee with one punch in the mouth. It looked as if he had knocked out every tooth in the poor guy's head.

The first thing I did was rush out on the floor and try to console the referee. The second thing I did was to tell the guys to hide Ralph until we could get him out of the country. If you hit anyone in Italy, it's a felony. There's no way to stay out of jail. Also, we could have been disqualified from playing in Italy and Ralph could have been kicked out of European basketball for life, which would have killed him.

I quickly called Gulf to explain what had happened. They said, "No matter what, we don't want any adverse publicity."

I visited the referee in the hospital and I couldn't have been more solicitous if it had been my mother in that bed. The guy was really hurt, but at the same time he knew who our sponsor was and that he had a chance to augment his referee's salary handsomely.

Eventually, we came to an agreement. We fixed up his teeth and, I think, his wardrobe, his front and back porches and a few outstanding bills. I don't really know what he did with the money, but either he had the most expensive dental repair bill of all time or he came out about $3,000 ahead. I didn't care, just as long as he didn't press charges.

We wound up paying a price of a different sort the next day, when we faced the Russians for the tournament championship. We led, 38–26, at the half and might have had a great victory if we had been playing only the Russians. But the officials had the previous day's game still fresh in their minds and reacted in belated defense of their injured colleague. We had nine free throws. The Russians had twenty-two. They won by eleven points.

This appears to be the place where I should do my number on the bane of the existence of every basketball coach. I will try to be fair. After all, some of my best friends are referees.

In the United States, the officiating varies from region to region. Fouls are called in the East in situations that are allowed in the Midwest, and so on. But this is nothing compared to the differences in referees around the world.

It seems to boil down to two factors: professionalism and style. Eastern European referees, for instance, are by and large quite impartial and expert. They have been taught what is permissible and what is not, and they follow the rules to the letter. The referees in the Philippines are also extremely fair under what can often be difficult circumstances.

In France, a country I expected more of, the officiating is generally poor. The referees there seem to be afraid of letting the game get out of control so they will call everything that could possibly be interpreted as a foul. My teams found it very difficult to adjust to this and it often detracted from our aggressive, fast-moving game. The worst homers I have ever seen may well have been in Israel. We played a game on a kibbutz and the referees, who lived there, seemed more anxious for the Israeli team to win than the fans did. In the cities, however, the refereeing was up to American standards—which is not surprising because the referees were Americans.

But it is in the Latin countries that you run into perhaps the most persistent partisanship. It's not so much that the referees there are dishonest as it is that they want to be noticed and applauded. The easiest way for a referee to be applauded is to call them for the home team. When this happens, it's because they want to be loved. The Latins crave the limelight and do things with style. Even traffic cops and waiters perform their jobs with a flourish. So do the referees. You can't really fight this—it's just a fact of life—but it makes for interesting situations when the referee is a fan of the local team.

There have been times when a referee has called a foul on a local star and then looked at him with a shrug and gesture of apology, which were then repeated in the direction of the coach. I have also seen a referee so overcome by a good play by the local team that he dropped his whistle and applauded. One of the most popular violations called against visiting teams is for being in the zone under the basket for more than three seconds. The purpose of this rule is to prohibit a player from just standing there and waiting for the ball, but some extremely innovative interpretations of it have developed. I have seen three seconds called on fast breaks, on jump balls, after rebounds and when we were on defense. It's been so bad that on some occasions, just to show my contempt, I have told my players to broad-jump across the zone so they won't touch the floor under the basket.

Another problem is the inability of the foreign referees to throw up a jump ball properly. I once saw a ball thrown so low that the opposing centers wound up slapping each other in the face. The game had to be delayed until the duel was over. Another time, the ball was thrown up too high and it looked as if the centers forgot about it, being in the third stage of the soul brothers' handshake by the time it came down. Happily, their thumbs were up at that point, the ball was deflected somewhere and the game went on.

It's easier for me to work on the referees when we are at a resort city and sunburned from a day at the beach. When I want to complain that a player has been pushed or hacked, I just tell the referee to look for fingerprints.

The problem of fast or slow thumbs on the timer's clock also comes up frequently. During one game in Belgium, I called a time-out with two minutes to go in the game. We got back on the court just as the buzzer went off. By the time I ran over to the scorer's table to protest, the timekeeper had packed up the clock and was on his way out of the building.

This is something that occurs in basketball the world over. The famous three-overtime game between Phoenix and Boston, in the finals of the 1976 NBA play-offs, almost certainly was stolen from Phoenix. The Boston timer wasn't about to put his finger on the button until it was convenient for the Celtics.

The key to dealing with the officials, I have found, is to try to remain as calm as possible. If they think they're getting to you, they love to rub it in. This can help set off the fans—who very often need very little help.

One of my best Gulf teams once made it to the finals of an important four-team tournament in Athens, where it met the Greek club champion, AEK. The game was played in the Olympic Stadium, the site of Greece's scientific win over Poland. By then, those days were gone forever—the visiting teams knew better than to start a game at the wrong time of the afternoon—but Greek teams still had an enviable record at home.

We were playing extremely well. With five minutes to go we had a 17-point lead, even though the referees were not only going for the homers-of-the-year award, but also were permitting a great deal of grabbing and holding, particularly on the part of the Greek star, a cocky hatchet man named Amerikanos. The Greek fans, all 10,000 of them, were seething because we were so far ahead. I think they might have joined us on the stadium floor if there hadn't been a fence separating us.

With only a few minutes remaining, the spark needed to turn this situation into a war was lit. Rod McDonald, one of my best players, stole the ball from Amerikanos, who was trying to pass it in bounds. The Greek player was furious and took a punch at Rod. He got four back in return and the battle was on. The two teams met angrily in the middle of the court and the fans began to push their way through and climb their way over the fence.

I thought we might be in for basketball's version of Custer's

Last Stand and go down surrounded by angry Greeks hurling abuse as well as more tangible missiles—like bottles. But at the last minute, the cavalry arrived. The Greek police, always ready for stadium rescues, pushed their way in just as we were about to put the wagon train in a circle and escorted us to a basement fortress, the scene of many such sieges in the past.

At the end, potential Greek tragedy turned into farce. After four hours in the dungeon, we headed back into town and found a restaurant. By purest chance, the entire Greek team was already there. They were well into the fourth course and their tempers had cooled in direct proportion to their stomachs being filled. We flew a white tablecloth to indicate a dinner-hour truce; by 2 A.M., we were all singing Greek songs.

The verbal abuse players are subjected to, particularly in Italy and the Latin American countries, takes a little getting used to. By an unwritten rule, the fans are allowed to say anything they like—about your family, your ancestry and your country—and the visitor must never respond. Break this rule and you let yourself in for a great deal of grief—as I can personally attest.

In 1968, I took a Gulf touring team to Puerto Rico where we played its national team, then preparing for the world championships. Right behind me, was a guy who jumped on me at the beginning of the game and never let up. I don't really mind being called old or fat or even an American. Nor was I too upset with the adjectives and adverbs he used in conjunction with these epithets. But the combination of them, ceaselessly repeated for forty minutes, did begin to wear on me after a while. My disposition wasn't improved by the referees, who seemed determined to boost the Puerto Rican team's confidence by calling an outrageously partisan game.

Somewhere near the end of the game, which was very close, one of my players got clobbered. When no foul was called, I stood up and started giving the referee hell. Behind me, my tormentor stood up and started giving me hell. I lost control, turned around and gave him the gesture known throughout the world as an invitation for him to perform an unnatural act upon himself. The crowd went mad, totally berserk, and I had to be escorted out of the arena by armed guards. I won't say that Puerto Ricans have long memories, but I haven't been invited back in the intervening ten years.

I responded to the fans on one other occasion—in Pesaro, Italy, the last time I coached an Italian club team. Pesaro is a town of about 50,000 people on the Adriatic with two distinctions as far as basketball was concerned. The population was crazy about the game and the officials fired the coach every January. I had been hired in January 1974 to replace a very popular coach who had been born and raised in Pesaro.

One local sportswriter decided he didn't like a single thing about me—my coaching methods, my outside interests or my personality—and this created some controversy. It was my fault, really. I had been in Italy long enough to know about the special circumstances of the press and how to handle them. Nearly all the papers represent some political point of view, which affects the way they report everything, even sports stories. The leftist press, for instance, will ask a newly arrived American if he hates being part of the exploited proletariat, which he usually doesn't understand even when he hears it translated into English. Or a reporter will ask how a player feels about solidarity. If the player says, "Yeah, teamwork is important," he will be quoted the next day as saying he backs the worker-student alliance.

In Pesaro, there was a battle between two groups for control of the basketball team that, in many ways, reflected the entire Italian political situation. One group was the Christian Democrats, most of them wealthy men; the other was tied to labor. The writer who took a dislike to me was part of the leftist press, not particularly disposed to supporting an American coach. It was my mistake not to cultivate him more than I did.

When the new season began in the fall, the criticism died down because the team was doing well. We were in third place in our division, but were very much in contention for the title because most of our early games had been played on the road. We would have the home-court advantage—which can be even more important in Italy than it is in the United States—for most of our remaining games.

One of our early losses had been to Chieti, now being coached by the man who had been fired from Pesaro the previous January. He had also obtained two of his former players, whom I had released in favor of some out-of-towners I had added to the team. So when time came for the return match, in January 1975, interest was high. The day before the game, an event occurred that turned the situation into a tinderbox. The former coach's father died. He had been a very popular figure in the town and there was an outpouring of sympathy for the exiled coach returning home. Not only were his players wearing black armbands when they arrived at the game, but the fans and even some of my players were, too.

The Chieti team was inspired, while we were understandably subdued. And I believe it is fair to say that the referees were just the tiniest bit cognizant of the situation and that some of their calls reflected this. Still, the game was close and everything went fairly smoothly, until I began to hear from one fan. He was upset that I wasn't using a player who had a lot of local support in place of one of my out-of-towners. And he told me so in loud, graphic terms. He kept up the harangue until the game was over —we were beaten by a point—and I lost my composure again. He got the same salute I had given the fan in Puerto Rico.

That tore it. All the latent hostility for the American interloper, who had taken the job of the grieving local man and who had brought in the outside players, was combined with the disappointment of losing this important game, and boiled over in a huge expression of fan resentment. I had to be hustled to a locker room and wait for four hours before I could leave the arena. This may have been unique in basketball history—a coach having trouble getting out of his own gym.

The next thing I knew, there was a meeting of the board of directors. For my own safety, they said, it might be just as well if I left town. I could hardly disagree, so the January firing tradition was upheld. It has been ever since, as a matter of fact.

There is one place where we received greater fan response than the home team—Singapore. The game was played in an amusement park called The Happy World. The basketball court was in the center of the park, which was jammed with people, and we quickly ran up a big lead over the local team. Soon, in fact, the promoter of the game, a member of the Chinese chamber of commerce, came up to me on the bench and said, "Coach, if you score a hundred points, it would be the greatest thing that ever happened to basketball in Singapore. It's never been done here before."

The closer we got to 100, the more the crowd began to cheer for us. With a few minutes left in the game, we hit it and you would have thought it was the Chinese new year. Rockets went off, cheers went up and the game was stopped. I was expecting a huge paper dragon to come out and dance on the floor. It was several minutes before the game was resumed. That was the only time I have ever felt sorry for the home team.

CHAPTER **22**

"Be Happy or Be Gone"

TURNING LOOSE a group of basketball players in Europe for the first time can often be an experience—for both the players and the continent. I curse the luck that let Mark Twain beat me to the use of the words "innocents abroad."

I had one player who showed up for the plane with a large canteen because of what he had heard about the water. He was surprised when I told him he was far better off drinking the water in Europe than that of his native Los Angeles.

Once we were sitting in an elegant patrician villa that had been converted into a hotel in Siena. There was a shimmering blue swimming pool nearby, a lovely garden beyond and white-gloved waiters to serve us. The players seemed to be acquiring a bit of taste almost by osmosis and were knowledgeably discussing an aspect of life in the city. Then one of them asked, "When are they going to finish demolishing that Coliseum in Rome?" Another said, "Why don't they do something about those big drainage ditches in Venice?" And a third said, "I really like those laundry basins they have in the bathrooms, though." He was talking about the bidets.

Yet, after a while, many of them began to fit right into the European scene, especially when it came to food. Here we had players raised on hamburgers and french fries, suddenly sniffing wines and ordering the best of European cuisine. I almost choked one day in a French restaurant when an inner-city kid sent back his *pâté de foie gras* for more seasoning.

Once in a while, a player will quit the tour because he's homesick. Sometimes, however, he departs for other reasons. During our 1977 travels, I was almost in tears listening to a player tell me how much he missed his aging grandmother and his working mother. We all bid him farewell with heavy hearts. Four days later, while driving through Geneva, we saw him pining away for home while sitting in a café with two pretty girls. If they were his mother and grandmother, they had found the fountain of youth.

One year, Julius Thigpen made the tour with us and, after a game in Paris, he went to take a look at Place Pigalle. Nearly every American who goes to France does this, but the difference between Julius and the others is that he didn't come back. The only way I knew he finally returned to the United States was when he showed up playing for the Detroit Pistons.

In all the years I've been taking players to Europe, I've had very few actual tourists. A lot of players would go to the Louvre or the Coliseum just to say they had been there, but there were very few who made a habit of going to the museums or the great cultural centers of Europe. Many seemed almost ashamed of being interested in anything that could be reasonably called highbrow.

I soon came to realize that most of them weren't in Europe to see Europe, but rather to play basketball. They had spent their whole lives doing that; it was the one thing they were good at and for which they got recognition. They didn't want to let go. This is hard for some people to understand. In a recent year, a French journalist joined us for a week to see what the tour was like. In many ways, his report in *L'Équipe* was accurate and favorable, but I felt he missed the point in his conclusion.

"I've been on the McGregor tour for a week," he wrote. "I've seen the trains, the hotels, the hurrying, the rough games, the difficult crowds, the unfair referees, the small reward. I found the boys to be delightful and McGregor to be interesting. I was able to do this for a week in pursuit of my profession, to write my report. But I wouldn't do it full time for all the tea in China."

What he didn't understand, I think, was the players' passion to play, their hunger for the game. For him, the end of the long train ride was a game to report, but it's different when that game is something you love. I, for instance, wouldn't, for any reason, put in eight hours a day of the contortions necessary to become a ballet dancer. But people who love ballet do it, even if no one outside their profession can understand.

There are times when I'm coaching that I get a feeling of euphoria nothing else gives me. Taking a group of young players and instilling hustle and desire in them can be like riding a huge wave that simply rolls along. There are periods when the preparation is right, the spirit is right, the timing is right and you have a sixth sense that everything is going to work. You seem to have a license from God that nothing can go wrong. It can all disappear in an instant, of course. Sometimes, a black cloud seems to be hanging over your head; nothing goes right. Eventually, you learn to live for the good moments.

So while the journalist was correct in observing the boring, difficult aspects of the tour, there was no way he could see how much it meant to those of us who loved it. There's the business aspect, but I would say that if they cut the salaries in Europe by fifty percent, there would still be 600 Americans playing there, just as there are today.

I have never instituted a lot of rules for the players, purely as a matter of survival. If you have rules, you must enforce them and for me it's not simply a matter of telling the offending party to hop a bus and go home. When the cost is an intercontinental plane ride, you try to live with your mistakes whenever possible. Still, there are several rules I have introduced over the years.

One of the most important is, No Questions of Any Kind. This was put into effect for my first touring team after I had been asked fifty times a day where the bathroom was. The players seemed astonished to learn that I didn't have a list of every bathroom in the world. So, we meet at one P.M. every day, at which time I tell them everything they need to know until one P.M. the following day. Except where the bathrooms are. For that, they're on their own.

The second basic rule is, Be Happy or Be Gone. There are so many problems connected with the tour—just getting from one place to another—that I simply don't have the time or the inclination to listen to money problems, woman problems or any other kind of problem. The complaint department, I tell the players, is closed and it is never going to open. If things aren't working out to their satisfaction, they are told at the beginning of the tour, they all have return-trip tickets and are welcome to use them. Once they're convinced that their problems are their own to solve, they usually manage just fine.

Their problems generally fall into a few basic categories. Lately, I have toyed with establishing a system of fines to cover them. It would go something like this:

$50 for every player who loses his uniform shirt to a girl who wants something to remember him by. It's touching to see Gulf, Gillette, Pepsi, Levi's and TWA shirts decorating the chests of the prettiest girls in Europe. But tradition and the goodwill of the sponsor require us to be wearing this year's shirt.

$100 for every player who asks me how to say, "What are you doing after the game tonight?" in the language of the country we are visiting.

$200 if the question is asked after I have just said, "Let's all get in early tonight because we have an early train in the morning."

$250 for missing the train. There are several variations of this. A player gets to the station on time, but grabs the train going north while we are going south. Or, he gets on the right train, but in the wrong car and is switched off to Germany while we head to Belgium. Or, forgetting that station stops last only ninety seconds, he throws his luggage off, but doesn't make it himself and continues on to the next stop, 100 miles down the line.

$500 for believing a sob story from the American veteran of a European club, whose job we are trying to take, about the loneliness and discrimination facing the American player in Europe where he is treated as a stereotyped athlete and not as the real person he is. This usually takes place a short distance from the veteran player's Mercedes, in which his girl friend is waiting to take him to the bar he is about to buy. Inasmuch as no one playing in Europe ever leaves of his own accord—unless a three-year, no-cut, NBA contract is waiting for him—it's hard to fall for this. But one or another of my players buys it every year.

Over the years, surprisingly few of my players have been in trouble with the law. This is something that continually concerns me because there's not much a foreigner can do once he gets caught up in the machinery of justice that prevails in many countries.

Most amazingly, none of my players has ever been arrested for carrying marijuana or other drugs. I warn the players constantly of the harsh penalties that prevail in Europe, particularly if they are caught with drugs while entering a country. And I say that not only will I not rush to their rescue if they are arrested, but I'll bribe the jailer to throw away the key. It's the kind of trouble I don't need.

Not until years later did players tell me that so-and-so had been smoking marijuana on the tour, or that I had missed a terrific hash party in Heidelberg, or that Quaalude had helped make bearable one particularly rough game in Varese. That would make me most aware of the generation gap. I could walk into a room full of people smoking marijuana and not recognize it.

The few brushes we have had with the law have been over things the players did, rather than what they smoked or swallowed.

Once in Belgium, in a suburb of Liège, we played in the afternoon, having made arrangements to check out of the hotel afterwards. The game was scheduled at one of those arenas that made it desirable to change at the hotel, but when the players returned there, still in uniform, they found their bags in the hall and their rooms locked because they were a few minutes late. I was still at the arena, talking with the promoter and reporters and picking up the check, so I wasn't around to help.

Several of the players began arguing loudly with the hotel owner, a little guy who argued right back. The discussion got pretty heated and one of the players picked up the man and hung him by the back of his shirt on a clothes hook. Give us the keys, the player said, and we'll let you down.

But the owner shouted to one of his people to call the police and within minutes the whole team had been hustled off to jail. When I arrived back at the hotel and learned what had happened, I chased down to the station house after them. I was hardly prepared for what I found. All of the players were sitting around, freshly showered, their bags neatly packed, having pleasant conversations with the police. In a moment, I was listening to the officer in charge apologize.

"I'm a big basketball fan," he said. "I've seen all the teams you've brought here and I thought it was best to get your players out of there by pretending to arrest them. We've had difficulties at that hotel before. So we put the players in cells long enough to use the showers and change their clothes. I'm terribly sorry for the inconvenience."

We even made our train to the next city.

One player who got into a couple of scrapes was Danny Rodriguez, a popular member of the tour in the late 1960s, who had been raised in the tough Mexican section of East Los Angeles and played at L.A. State. Danny was a fine player of only average height, but with great speed and combativeness, and the crowds loved him. However, he had a knack for finding trouble, and having it find him.

Once he went to a nightclub in Madrid with Dennis Gray, who was his exact opposite—big, blond and slow. Somehow or other, Danny got into an argument with a waiter which led to an exchange of pushes, which led to an exchange of punches, which led to the police being called. The first thing you learn in most altercations of this type is that the foreigner is generally wrong. But Danny didn't wait to find out.

He took off with what appeared to be enough of a headstart that nobody would catch him. Just to make sure, he zigged and zagged down different streets to lose anyone who might be on his trail. But nobody was following him; they were all after Dennis Gray. Not having been involved in the fight, Dennis had set off leisurely for the hotel. The police, told that he and Danny had been together, had leisurely followed him. Dennis led them straight to the hotel where they arrested Danny, whose city-bred talents for escape had all been for nothing. I managed to get him out of jail, for which he was properly grateful.

On the same tour, Danny got into another scrape that he didn't want any help with. We were in Hälsingborg, Sweden, staying at a youth center where they shut the doors at a certain time, and Danny got back late one night. He pressed the buzzer, waking up the caretaker who came down in his nightshirt. Instead of opening the door all the way, the caretaker just cracked it and pointed at the clock. Danny was so disgusted that he picked up a stick and threw it at the quarter-inch opening. His aim was better than his luck. The stick went through and hit the caretaker on the nose. Once again, Danny was hauled off to jail.

As it happened, they had just built a nice new jail in Hälsingborg with a movie, a workshop, a newsstand and a barber shop—all the comforts of home. The only thing they lacked was inmates. Danny was greeted with open arms. The jailer was happy to have someone in jail, the cook was happy to have someone to cook for and the other prison employees treated him like royalty, too. When I arrived with some of the other players to bail out Danny, he would have none of it.

"What do you mean, get me out? Back on that lousy tour. Games every night, travel all day, lousy hotels that won't even let you in at night."

He played it to the hilt and we were all crying with laughter. I think some of the other players wouldn't have minded trading places with him. In the end, they turned Danny loose, still protesting that he wanted to stay.

If Danny's scrapes were relatively harmless, there was one player on the tour with a flair for trouble of a much more serious nature. His name doesn't matter—let's call him Jack Harvey—but the problems he caused did. Jack, who was from a midwestern college with a good record, showed up at the tryout camp for my second Gulf touring team. He was a six-foot-eight forward and a good player, but a little slow and not quite strong enough to make that team, which was a fine one.

After the work-out, I told him the bad news and he asked me to come out to his car. It was clear from the mess that he had been sleeping in it and soon he was showing me his scrapbook with clippings of his high-school and college exploits. I could hardly believe it. The guy not only looked like a country bumpkin, he acted like one, too. Here he was, surrounded by top draft choices and All-Americans, and he was showing me clippings of his prep days in Santa Fe.

Then something else in his car attracted my attention—personalized pool cues, the kind that are kept in a small box and screwed together when used.

"I'm a hustler," Jack said, when I asked what they were. "I make my living hustling. Pool, cards, anything. I love basketball and I really want to play, but hustling is how I live."

I went away, somehow glad that I would never see him again. I couldn't have been more mistaken.

At every tryout camp for the next two or three years, Jack would show up. And everywhere I went around the world, he would track me down by telephone. I would be in a hotel and there would be a call for me, or I would be walking through an airport and hear myself paged. From the first word, I knew who it was.

"Coach," he would say, in a long whining drawl I grew to hate, "This is Ja-a-ack. I'd sure like to be with you, Coach. I'm playing better. Give me another chance. You're a good Christian coach. You know I can play. You know."

Not long after I first started getting these calls, I began hearing from the telephone company.

"Do you remember getting a call from the United States on such-and-such a date?" they would ask.

"I make my living on the telephone. I can't remember every call."

"Well, the calling party was a Jack Harvey."

"Oh, yes. I sure remember that one."

"We're trying to find him."

"Well, I'm not. I'm trying to get away from him."

It was clear that he was using telephone credit cards illegally or making calls from the houses of people who thought he was their friend. This happened at least a dozen times.

One summer, a few years after I met Jack, I was in Los Angeles and went to see Bill Sharman. We had been friends since attending USC together and he was then coaching the L.A. Stars of the ABA.

"I've got this guy following me around all the time," Bill said. "He's not a bad player, but I can't use him. Can you take him on the tour, get him a job in Europe?"

"I bet I know his name," I said. "Jack Harvey."

"You're right," Bill said. "I can't turn the corner without him being there."

It was then that I made my big mistake. The ABA had cut deeply into my talent pool in the previous few years and many of the players I was taking to Europe were no longer as good as Jack. He soon found out I was in Los Angeles and made another plea to join the tour. Against my better judgment, I agreed.

For a while, things went smoothly. Jack played well, got along with the other players despite a lot of bragging and tall stories and didn't seem to be causing any trouble. I began to wonder if I had misjudged him. Then Jack made the mistake of trying to cheat another player, Tom Thomas, in a poker game. Tom, one of my favorite players, had grown up on the streets of St. Louis. Apparently, his father had run some sort of gambling operation and Tom knew everything there was to know about cards and about cheating at them. It was a classic case of the professional gambler meeting his match.

Usually, our poker games on the tour were nickel-and-dime stuff, just a way to pass the time. But Tom liked high-stakes card games as much as Jack did and turned out to be a far superior player. Jack used every trick he knew, but Tom kept one step ahead of him all the way. One night in Rome, Jack wound up owing Tom $300.

"Gee, I went in a little over my head," Jack said, with his best little-boy grin. "I don't have that kind of money."

I didn't have the slightest doubt about Jack's story. It was typical of him not to let a little thing like his inability to pay up keep him out of a card game if he thought he could cheat enough to win. Jack soon had everybody convinced that he didn't have another dime. Everybody except Tom.

"Jack," he said, "if you want to get out of this room alive, you're going to pay me and you're going to pay me now."

"I haven't got it, Tom," Jack said, almost whining. "I'm sorry. I just can't pay you."

Tom picked up a large bottle, got up and walked over to where Jack was sitting.

"That's enough, Tom," I said. "Let's not have any trouble. You can see he doesn't have the money."

"Coach," Tom said, "I know what I'm doing. Don't worry about it. You guys just take off if you want to. I'm going to beat it out of this guy if I have to, but I'm going to get the money."

A few of the players did leave the room, but Tom didn't notice. He never took his eyes off Jack.

"Now, come up with it," he said, "or I'm going to tear you apart."

Jack sat there for a moment, then he took off his shoe. He dug down inside and pulled out three $100 bills. He had the money, Tom knew he had it and I think he knew Tom would probably beat him senseless if he didn't hand it over. They had read each other perfectly.

That incident seemed to quiet Jack down for a little while. There were no more card games, no more bragging, no more hustling. Then one night, about a month later, I was asleep in my hotel room in Zagreb when there was a loud knock on the door.

I sat up, rubbing the sleep from my eyes as I asked who it was.

"Police," came the answer. "Please open."

Damn, I thought, while I fumbled for the light and a bathrobe. Yugoslavian police in the middle of the night. This has to be bad trouble.

"We have a player of yours in the jailhouse," the uniformed officer said when I opened the door.

"What did he do?"

"He made a long-distance call from a hotel and didn't pay for it."

"But I've given instructions to the hotel that no phone calls are authorized unless they're paid for in advance. That's something I do everywhere we go."

"He went to another hotel, the Intercontinental, placed a long-distance call to America and then ran away."

I no longer had any doubts who it was. I got dressed and went down to the police station. If I were in a jail in a communist country, I would be frightened to death. But when I saw Jack, it was obvious that, to him, a jail was a jail. He was sure he could talk his way out of this one, the way he must have done back home.

"Coach, it was all a misunderstanding," he said. "It was a collect call."

I tried to tell this to the police officer, with whom I'd been talking in German, but the word for collect would not come to me. Finally, with a little sign language, I got the idea through and the policeman agreed to take us back to the Intercontinental.

"This man said he placed his call collect," I told the hotel operator. "Maybe you didn't understand. I'm sure this can be straightened out."

The hotel manager—at least he spoke English—was also in on the conversation and said, "Then why did he run away?"

I had no answer for that as I tried to picture this six-foot-eight hulk trying to make his way inconspicuously into the Yugoslavian night. But at last he agreed to let Jack make the call again, to see if the person on the other end would accept the charges.

Jack stood outside the phone booth, giving it his best shot. He squirmed around, holding the receiver a little way from his ear so I could hear both ends of the conversation as I stood next to him.

"Honey, remember that collect call I placed?" Jack sweet-talked to the poor woman—I never did find out who she was—on the other end of the line.

"You son of a bitch, I wouldn't take a collect call from you if you were in the electric chair," she said.

"Oh, honey—she's all shook up, coach. She doesn't know what she's saying. There's been a tragedy in the family. Would you talk to her, explain everything?"

I took the telephone and said, "Listen, I know that it wasn't a collect call and I know that you're not going to pay for it and I have a sinking feeling that I'm going to pay for it or he's going to be stuck in this communist jail—."

"I'm not going to tell anybody in the whole wide world that this was a collect call and wind up with the bill," she said. "I didn't want to hear from him in the first place. He's conned me for the last time."

"I'm Jim McGregor, his coach—"

"You may be Jim McGregor and you may be some con-man friend of his."

"Look, as much as I'd like him to go to jail and stay there, it would be very bad publicity for me. Even if I pay cash for the call, he's not off the hook because he made it and ran. Please, just do this. Call a friend of mine in Los Angeles in a little while and tell him I agreed to pay you for the call. In the meantime, I'll call him and okay it and you'll have the money right away. But right now, please, please, say that it was a collect call."

"God, I'm getting conned again," she said. "I can feel it."

Finally she agreed, I put the manager on the telephone, and she said, yes, it had been a collect call.

By now the cost of the original call and this one added up to $200. As we went back to our hotel, I said, "Jack, I want that money right now."

"Coach, I haven't got two hundred dollars."

"Jack, I don't know how to get two hundred dollars out of you, but I know a guy who does. I'm going to tell Tom that you're into me for two hundred and if I don't get the money within half an hour, it's going to be four hundred. You know Tom's just been waiting for another chance at you."

He thought a minute and said, "Yeah, coach, you're right."

By then, we knew all about his shoe trick, so he had a new hiding place—inside a compartment at the back of his belt. He took the belt off, pulled out the money and handed it over.

The next day, in front of the team, I said, "Jack, I'm getting rid of you before you get us all thrown in jail. The moment we get back to Greece, you're gone."

And Jack, just as cool as he could be—as if nothing out of the ordinary had happened—said, "Well, I'm thinking of going back and trying out for the NBA anyway, coach."

Tom, who had heard the whole story along with everyone else, said, "I'll tell you what, you son of a bitch, for every minute you ever play in the NBA, I'll give you twenty bucks."

"I'll cover that bet, too," somebody said and pretty soon everybody on the team was in on it.

"Don't," Jack said. "I'm going to make it."

As long as we were in Yugoslavia, we had to stay together and it was several days before we returned to Greece. Until then, Jack did everything he could to stay on the tour. He begged and pleaded and asked for just one more chance. But when we got to the Athens airport to catch a flight to Italy, I had made up my mind. Now I had to figure out a way to get rid of him.

"Jack," I said, a few minutes before our plane was to take off, "I want you to get me a couple of newspapers and bring them to me on the plane. We leave from Gate Eight."

Jack headed for the newsstand. Moments later, we stood on the steps of the boarding ramp at Gate 7. When I saw that they were about to shut the plane door, we all waved across the runway, shouting, "Yoo-hoo, Jack!" and ran up the steps. The door shut behind us and we took off.

I have no idea how Jack got out of Athens or where he went, but I had complete confidence that, one way or another, he would be able to take care of himself. Eventually, he did get back to the United States and, in fact, he did play for an NBA team for part of a season. He never asked anybody to pay off the bet, though.

Even that was not the end of it. Five or six years later, I saw Jack for the last time. I was flying back to the United States from Germany and he was on the same plane.

"My God, Jack, what are you doing here?" I said.

And as if nothing had ever happened between us, he said, "Coach, I've been playing for Munich in the European Pro League [a short-lived venture formed by American promoters]. I wasn't getting enough playing time and I didn't get along with the coach, so I'm going back home."

There was no help for it but to sit and chat on the long plane ride. At one point, I asked him why he did the things that were always getting him into trouble: writing bad checks, placing fraudulent long-distance phone calls, running out on his debts. His answer was a classic.

"Coach, they ask for it. They just wave it in front of me. They have it coming. By the way, I have this travel voucher from the team in Munich that will get me to the West Coast, but I'm going to stay in New York and I can use the cash. Do you want to buy it from me?"

I must have been crazy even to think about it, but if there

was one thing I knew about, it was airline tickets, and since I was going home to Portland with a few stops along the way, I took a look at the voucher. It was all paid for, completely valid.

"Jack," I said, "the only reason I'd buy this voucher from you would be to save money. It's worth seven hundred dollars. I'll give you six hundred for it."

When we landed in New York, I took the voucher to the airline counter to check it out absolutely. The ticket agent assured me that it was good, and I wrote Jack a check. He disappeared from my sight for the last time and I breathed a sigh of relief. Then I looked at the voucher again. It was in his name.

It was still good, but I would have to fly from New York to Miami to Los Angeles to Portland and back to New York again under the name of Jack Harvey. All I could think of for the next month of my travels was what would happen if the plane crashed. Nobody would know that it was me who had died and not Jack. Which would, I suppose, have been a fitting end to our relationship.

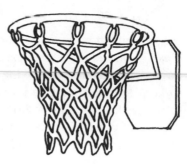

CHAPTER 23

Missing Persons and a Day in the NBA

IN THE LATE 1960s, I stumbled into a different line of work totally by accident. Late one night, I was asleep in my apartment in Rome when the telephone rang. It was a good friend of mine who was a successful businessman in California. It was for neither business nor friendship that he was calling, though.

"Jim!" I heard him yell as, half awake, I picked up the telephone. "For God's sake, get down and help my daughter."

I had to slow him down long enough to find out who it was.

"My daughter's in Rome," he said, "at a *pensione* on the Via Veneto, and she just called me and said there's a guy outside her door trying to break in."

"Let me get this straight," I said. "She's in Rome and she phones you in California—"

"She said she couldn't get a local call through," he broke in.

Now he was beginning to make sense. The Rome telephone service is so unreliable that it's often easier to call around the world than next door. So I jumped into my car, rushed down to the Via Veneto, woke up the manager of the *pensione* and ran to the girl's room.

Sure enough, a local Lothario had followed her around that

evening and now was showing his regard for her by trying to break down her door. One look at him and I could see there was no real danger. He was trying to prove that nothing was going to keep him and his true love apart. But the girl was frightened so we yelled at him a little, threatening to call the police. That cooled off his ardor enough to send him home. The girl soon calmed down and within an hour I was back in my room, asleep.

But that was just the beginning. My friend's business took him up and down the West Coast and he met a lot of people. For months, I guess, his favorite topic of conversation was the night his daughter had called him from Rome and I had rushed over to save her from a fate worse than death. I'm sure he embellished the story with vivid details and soon I was getting calls from dozens of distraught parents.

"We heard what a great thing you did," they would say. "Well, our daughter's over in Europe, too, and we haven't heard from her in months. Can you help us?"

Often, they would be crying as they spoke, and it was pretty hard to convince them that there was nothing I could do. So I would get a description and whatever details they could give me and promise to try to help.

The calls kept coming and they were so tearful and plaintive that I couldn't get them out of my mind. Then one day it hit me. I had contacts all over Europe well equipped to help find missing kids: basketball players, both those on the tour and those I had placed in jobs in years past. Nearly all of them hung out where they knew they would find other Americans. The American Express office, where everybody went to get money from home, was popular and so were places where players could get hamburgers, milkshakes and, I suppose, marijuana.

So pretty soon I started telling the distraught parents who called that, yes, I did have a sort of organization that would help to find runaway kids. I saw no reason to say that the "organization" was nothing more than a bunch of basketball players on the loose, but I doubt it would have mattered. The parents were almost prostrate with gratitude at the thought that somebody would actually be looking for their kids.

Before long, I had a list of runaways that I sent out to players all over Europe. The list included names, descriptions and last-known whereabouts. The players were eager to help, but only up to a point. If they found a kid on the list, they would tell him or her to call home, but that would be the end of it. They weren't going to put the finger on anybody who didn't want to be found. That was the code of ethics they felt they had to follow.

I had my doubts about how well this would work because I assumed the missing kids wouldn't cooperate. But the opposite turned out to be true. Most of them desperately wanted to be found. All they had to do was pick up the phone and say, "Hi, Mom," but they wanted someone to find them first and take them to the phone so they could say, "Oh, Mom, I'm sorry."

Each time we found a runaway, the story would be spread even farther in the United States. We must have found five or ten kids in each of the next five years and soon we were charging $500 plus expenses. We were never at a loss for business; in the late sixties and early seventies, there were armies of kids running all over Europe. Often, the ones we found weren't really runaways at all, but had just forgotten to call home for a while. As soon as a player spotted them by their descriptions, it was easy to persuade them to get on the phone.

It wasn't always that simple. A couple of kids turned out to be in jail and more than a few were in real trouble. This was especially true of the flower children who may have been full of peace and love themselves, but were just lambs ripe for the slaughter by the wolves who were prowling around Europe.

There was one girl in particular we were quite worried about. Her picture and description made her appear rather plain and dumpy, but she looked awfully good at the bank. She had a lot of money in a checking account and all she had to do was walk into an American Express office, write a check and be on her way. Soon the checks were being cashed much more often than usual and by the time her parents called us she had dropped out of sight completely. She had been seen last in Amsterdam so I sent word to two of my players who were there.

One was Gerhardt Schreur, a huge guy from Arizona State and one of the strongest I have ever had on the tour. He was very placid, never displaying any temper, but I wouldn't have wanted to be around if he did. His running mate was Bill More, from Oregon, who was just the opposite—friendly, talkative and something of a flower child himself. Shortly after I told them to watch out for the missing girl, they wandered into the American Express office in Amsterdam with her picture and there she was.

Bill walked right up and said he had been looking for her. She seemed a little frightened, but confirmed her identity. Just then a big guy approached from a little way off and said, "Run along, boy. None of your affair here."

The man looked very menacing, but his expression changed quickly when Gerhardt walked over, towering over the whole group.

"What's not our affair?" he said, and before the guy could answer, the girl burst into tears and threw herself into Bill's arms.

"You've got to help me," she sobbed. "Get me away from him." She wrapped herself around Bill and cried and cried.

The guy took one more look at Gerhardt, mumbled something about how he was only kidding, and split. It turned out he had actually kept her locked in a room, only letting her out long enough to go down to American Express and cash checks. Before that, she had taken him all over Europe, bought him clothes and a car and given him a lot of money.

When she told us her story, we asked her if she wanted to press charges, but she said, "No, I just want to get away." I think she was very happy to leave Europe.

There were times when our missing-persons operation took unusual twists. On at least four or five occasions, we ended up working, not for parents who wanted their kids back, but for husbands who were looking for their wives and vice versa.

One day, a woman called from the United States and said, "Are you Jim McGregor, the finder?"

"I'm Jim McGregor, the basketball coach," I said. "On occasion, I help find people over here through my organization."

"Can you find a son of a bitch?" she said.

"Uh—any other description?"

"Yeah, he's my husband and he's a masochist."

"Well, that's a pretty good clue. Send me a picture and some information about him and tell me what I'm supposed to do if I find him."

"Well, don't send him back. I just want to find him and get a message to him."

Knowing a person's habits gives a pretty good head start when you set out to find him. If a man is homosexual, it's usually easy to hunt him down if you know what city he's in because there are gay bars everywhere. A lot of people who go to Europe to escape from something have strongly defined compulsions or interests. Like basketball, I suppose. Anyway, I knew exactly where to start looking for my masochist.

Once, on a train, I had sat next to a woman who had become notorious when she was expelled from the United States for running a house of sadism. Her customers were supposed to be well-known, important men, although none of their names ever leaked out. She had told me about many of her adventures and I remembered she mentioned advertising in a Dutch newspaper. I called up a reporter I knew and asked for her phone number.

"Oh, yes," she said when I called. "Basketball coach Jim McGregor. We had a nice train ride. You need whipping, maybe?"

"No, no, nothing like that," I said. "I just wanted—"

"What do you like?" she interrupted. "Chains, enemas, stuff like that?"

"No, I'm trying to find a man."

"Aren't we all?"

"This guy's a masochist."

"Oh, that won't take long."

I gave her a description and she gave me phone numbers in

about five European cities. Of course, everyone I called had the same question: "What's in it for me?"

So I called back the guy's wife and asked, "How much reward will you offer? I have to split this with three or four people who are helping me."

"How about a thousand dollars?" she said.

Hell, for a thousand dollars, I'd have joined the guy on his hunt for the perfect torture. I spread the word about the money.

Sure enough, a woman in Hamburg, where there's a whole nest of these places, called and said he was there.

"Don't let him get away," I said.

"Don't worry," she said. "I've got him chained up. That's part of the act."

"Good," I said. "No matter what he's paying you, keep him there."

"Are you kidding? He's in seventh heaven."

So I called the guy's wife and told her where he was.

"That's his thing, all right," she said. "Make sure he stays there for twenty four hours. I want to send my attorney over."

For that, I got the better part of $1,000. It was an interesting sideline.

This was not my only occupation away from the tour and the transferring of players in the last decade. There was also my NBA career, a meteoric one as long as it lasted. Which was one day.

In 1970, I had taken a touring team to Hong Kong and I was in my hotel room when the phone rang. The caller identified himself as Sam Schulman, a name that meant nothing to me. I had been out of the United States for some time and, though I had kept up with the NBA players and coaches, I hadn't kept track of all of the owners. Schulman had to identify himself as the owner of the Seattle SuperSonics.

I was digesting that information when he said, "How would you like to be my general manager?"

I was sure this was somebody down in the lobby of the hotel, pulling my leg, but I decided to go along with it. Sure, I would be interested, I said. Why not?

"Tell me the conditions you would propose," he said.

"Well, I'd want fifty thousand dollars a year and a chance to participate in any increased earnings I could bring to the club while I was general manager."

"That sounds reasonable. If I send you a ticket, can you come and talk with me at once?"

I said I could, hung up the phone and waited for a bunch of my players to come bursting through the door, laughing about how I had fallen for their trick.

But then the phone rang again. "This is Pan American Airlines," a voice said. "We have a prepaid ticket for you to fly from Hong Kong to Los Angeles and Seattle and return. Would you like to book your flight?"

"What's your number?" I said, still not believing any of it. "I'll call you back."

And, by God, it *was* Pan Am. And they *did* have a ticket for me. I didn't know anybody prepared to spend $1,500 on a practical joke, so twelve hours after Schulman had called, I was flying to Los Angeles. Waiting for me there were a limousine and a uniformed chauffeur.

"We've made reservations for you at the Beverly Hilton," the driver said, "but Mr. Schulman asks if you could come directly to his office."

I certainly could.

We arrived at the National General Corporation, where I was ushered through a battery of receptionists and secretaries, each one more beautiful than the last. I was ready to take the job with no further discussion if I didn't have to leave the building or give up the chauffeur. Finally, I made it to the top floor where I was greeted by Schulman in an office with a breathtaking view of the city. He got right down to business.

"I've been forced to change my general manager at Seattle because of some disagreements," he said. "I've decided I need a man with some knowledge of the Northwest and I've made some inquiries. You've been recommended to me. I find the conditions you propose acceptable and I'd like you to go to Seattle tomorrow to meet with my board of directors."

We were joined then by Schulman's business partner, Eugene Klein, who owned the San Diego Chargers pro football team. Both men had started as used-car salesmen and five minutes in the presence of their confidence and authority showed me why there are three million used cars sold every year.

I felt obliged to point out that, although I had been in basketball all my life, I had been away from the game in the United States for over a decade and had no experience at all in the NBA. I would have to do a lot of studying to learn the rules and procedures, but I thought I knew talent, was a good promoter and would be well received in the Northwest.

"That's precisely the reason that led me to decide to offer you this position," Schulman said. "I've talked to Red Auerbach about it."

That puzzled me because I knew Auerbach, the general manager of the Boston Celtics, only slightly and was surprised that he would recommend me. The next day, I was in Seattle for what Schulman had said would be the formality of being named general manager of the SuperSonics.

But the moment I walked into the team's offices, I learned that all was not as it was supposed to be. The board of directors was. in revolt against Schulman because he had fired Dick Vertlieb as general manager. Vertlieb had done a good job for the Sonics, building up interest and attendance in the expansion franchise. His break with Schulman had occurred because he had given his word on a player deal and Schulman hadn't backed him up.

"You've had a long trip," said one of the Portland board members, "and we understand the commitment that's been made to you. This should not in any way be taken as prejudicial to you, but we have made an offer to Bob Houbregs, a local man, and we're pretty well united in thinking that he should be engaged and that we should put some limit on the authority of Mr. Schulman."

"I didn't seek this position," I said. "I was invited here and I'm very happy to be considered, but if you've made a decision, why, I'll just return to my own business."

I called Schulman and told him what had happened. As much as he would like to, he said, he could not fire the whole board. I should stop to see him in Los Angeles on my way back to Hong Kong.

This time, there was no limousine at the airport and, though the receptionists hadn't changed, I had a long wait before getting in to see Schulman. When I did, the used-car dealer had given way to Hollywood producer.

"I regret what happened," he said very brusquely. "Here's a letter for you." The only thing he didn't say was, "Don't call me. I'll call you."

I was still curious about how he had chosen me, in the first place. It turned out that when he had asked Auerbach to recommend a local man, Red had said he didn't know any, but he did know someone who did—Jack Nichols. Nichols had played on the Celtics under Auerbach for a few years and was then a dentist in Seattle. We had gone to USC together and had remained friends. On the basis of two telephone calls, the direction of a million-dollar business had almost been placed in my hands.

After I left Schulman's office for the airport, I remembered the envelope and looked inside. There was a check for $1,000. I figured that was adequate compensation for my time.

CHAPTER 24

Ladies of the Tour

ONE CONSTANT of the tour was women. The players and the girls of Europe were continually discovering each other, to the mutual delight of both.

They met each other in the trains, on the beaches and in the discotheques, but most of all at the games themselves. By some remarkable coincidence, the girls could always be found hanging around the locker rooms. They would ask for an autograph, the player would offer his room number as well as his signature, and that would be the beginning of a beautiful friendship.

This created a bit of a problem for me, however. Very few single men on the loose carried around their own unbeatable competition. Here I was, getting older, paunchier and balder by the year, having to compete with ten or twelve young men who were tall, handsome and in the prime of life. But I did have one advantage unavailable to the players—my airlines pass. I still represented various airlines because of the free transportation and the money I could make, but such a position had other uses as well.

Suppose there were a few days between games in Sweden during a cold or rainy period. In a conversation with a young lady, I might find the standard question—"Would you like to have dinner with me tomorrow?"—eliciting no particular interest. But when it was followed by the words, "in Rio de Janeiro," the response was often very different. A few years often came off my age and a few pounds off my middle.

Generally, the tour has some favorite places as far as the availability of women is concerned and Paris is always one of them. I would like to report that the American players are a big hit with the French girls—and they might well be if they gave them a chance. But as soon as the players hit town, the word spreads about where all the English-speaking students are hanging out. Usually it is a club on the Left Bank—in recent years it has been the Concord, the Top Banana and Mother Earth—and that's where they spend the bulk of their evenings. I may be the only coach in the world who knows exactly where every member of his team is at three in the morning.

As far as the Mediterranean is concerned, its reputation as a bachelor's paradise of sea, sand, sun and willing ladies is not altogether deserved. Except for the hustler, a common denominator of every society, you can forget the women of Italy, Greece, Turkey and, most of all, any of the Arab countries. Not counting the English, German, Scandinavian and American women who vacation on the Riviera, there's really only one Mediterranean country where the women have the same liberated attitude as those in northern Europe and the United States—Israel. Going to Israel from a nearby country—usually Greece or Turkey—is something we all look forward to. The fact that many of my former players have settled there and are happy to show us some hospitality, makes it all the nicer.

As I've said before, however, the most eagerly awaited part of the tour is Sweden. One of the unique things about Swedish basketball is that the officials at the scorer's table—the score-keepers, the timer and the person counting the fouls—are generally female. They may be members of the club that has organized the game or they may be on a women's team. But the fact that they are there makes reporting into the game of more than routine interest to the players.

"I'm going in for number five and how about going out with you after the game?" is the usual approach.

The first time we visited Malmö, in 1969, there were three attractive girls working at the scorer's table. By the time the first half was over, the starting front line—the center and both forwards—had dates for the evening. Much to our surprise, the three girls followed us around on the remainder of our tour in Sweden, permanently attached to the center and the two forwards.

The next year, I took another team to Sweden and, when we got to Malmö, there were the three girls at the scorer's table again. I don't know whether they were looking for the same three players, but, on finding out they weren't with us, the trio made quick substitutions. The girl who'd gone with the center the year before picked my new starting pivot man. The other two went for the starting forwards. And, once again, they followed us around Sweden.

This happened for the next three or four years. Somewhere along the way they were dubbed the Andrews Sisters and became a legend of the tour. I sometimes wondered why nobody ever offered me a bribe to be put on the starting front line when we got to Malmö. It may be that nobody on the team ever really lacked for feminine company in Sweden if he wanted it.

For some reason, players travelling with girls to whom they weren't married seldom presented any major problems. It was the wives—both the ones left at home and those who came along —who made trouble of one kind or another. We've had everybody from the Dragon Lady, constantly fomenting strife, to the Honeymoon Shouter, keeping the whole tour awake at night with her cries of marital bliss. The 100-year-old hotels in which we stay don't have walls thick enough for newlyweds. In 1977, one player brought along his bride, and one night they put on such a performance that an entire hotel corridor erupted with applause. I think they're preparing to name their first child Encore.

Wives at home often present bigger problems. I've been awakened in the middle of the night by women in the United

States demanding to know where their husbands are. Usually, they are players who haven't been on the tour for more than a year. My stock answer is, "I can't keep track of my own wife, much less your husband."

Then there are the letters that come in:

> Dear Mr. McGregor:
> Can you help me reach Tom Terrific? You may remember me. I was with him for a while about two months ago. I have some news for him. Please let him know that he must contact me or my brothers will be contacting him.
>
> Thank you
> Miss Distress

Several years ago, one player kept boring everybody with the story of how much his wife loved him and missed him and worried about him when he was gone. After a week of this, we thought a conversation with her might shut him up for a while so we all chipped in to pay for a telephone call. His wife wasn't home. He tried several times more that night, with the same results. By then, several of the players were hanging around the telephone while he called her family, his family, neighbors and friends. Nobody knew where she was. So the team came up with some suggestions.

"Have you tried the TV repairman?" they wanted to know. "Her lawyer? Your lawyer? The milkman? The neighborhood dyke?"

This went on for two and a half days, with him continually trying to reach her and the guys ribbing him unmercifully. Finally, he got so shook that one night he just disappeared. We never found out where his wife was. I wonder if he did.

I have been married twice, have had a couple of long-standing relationships and have made the dubious gift of my attentions to women around the world. Yet the only part of this I truly regret is that I allowed my first marriage to die.

Diane and I met at USC when I was the freshman track coach and she was an undergraduate. She was lovely, personable, editor of the yearbook—all in all, much too good for me. After we had been seeing each other quite a lot, I tried to get up enough courage to ask her to marry me, but I don't think my proposal was as forthright as it might have been. We were at a track meet, seated on cold benches and she was eating a hot dog, which was as close to a candlelit dinner as I could afford at the time.

"Well, if you're going to be a coach's wife," I said, "I guess you'll have to get used to hot dogs and bleachers."

Perhaps this proposal made up in sincerity what it lacked in eloquence, but at any rate it was accepted and I was delighted. The job at Whitworth came shortly after we were married and it is easy to see now that I began to shut her out of my life immediately. I was so wrapped up in being a coach and athletic director—recruiting, organizing, building my team—that I hardly thought of her at all. I know I was happy that dinner was ready, that the house was in order and that I had an attractive wife on my arm at the proper occasions. That she might have some needs and desires deserving as much consideration as mine never occurred to me. Before long, love went out the window, with me giving it a healthy boost.

It was years later before I married again. I met Barbara aboard the *Queen Mary*, which was cruising the Mediterranean at the time. I often spent my vacations as a lecturer aboard ships in Europe. This may seem to be a real busman's holiday—taking a vacation from travelling by travelling—but actually it was quite relaxing. I wasn't always packing my bag, I got a chance to meet people and, besides, it didn't cost anything.

We had stopped at the island of Madeira on our way over from New York, and, while most of the crew went ashore, I stayed up on the sun deck at the pool. Suddenly, I found I had a lot of company. A group of German tourists was being taken around the ship as part of a travel-agency tour. What interested me most was their guide. She was much younger than I was and made Anita Ekberg look pale and scrawny.

I asked her to have a drink with me on the sun deck while her tour browsed around the ship. She was as friendly and easy to talk to as she was attractive and soon I found myself thinking of the stories I had heard as a kid in Portland about sailors who had been shanghaied. There was a club in the harbor where, in the old days, they would lure in unsuspecting fellows with the promise of a few drinks, get them drunk and drop them down in the hold of a whaleboat. By the time they woke up, they were on the high seas. With each passing drink, it occurred to me what an excellent idea that seemed.

When Barbara's tour was supposed to leave the ship, she said, "I really must go back."

"I'm sure they can find their way to the hotel," I said. "Why don't you stay on board?"

While she protested she had to leave, she didn't get up from her deck chair and pretty soon the discussion became academic. The tour was long gone. My next project was to talk her into staying on the ship. Women can find a million reasons not to do what they know they shouldn't do, and this was no exception. She had no overnight kit, no change of clothes and so forth. But with each additional drink there seemed to be one less reason for her departure. Pretty soon, we both noticed a rocking sensation. We looked around and saw the harbor of Madeira receding in the distance. We were at sea. Which is how I shanghaied my second wife.

Actually, it didn't all happen quite that quickly. Barbara did get back to Madeira after a few days to find that she had been fired. We saw a great deal of each other for the next year or so and decided to get married. This wasn't quite as easy as it sounds, though. I was a resident of Italy and we wanted to get married there. The first thing we discovered was that one of the Italian laws required me to certify that Barbara was in no way involved in my previous divorce. A bit of rapid calculation revealed that at the time I was divorced from Diane, Barbara had been only three years old; so that problem was solved.

The paperwork involved in marrying a German citizen to an American living in Italy was so complicated that finally we just gave it up, telling our friends we had eloped so that they could go through with the wedding reception and parties they had arrranged. Then, when ostensibly we were flying away for our honeymoon, we went instead to that sentimental capital of romance, Las Vegas, and got married there. Nothing like doing things backwards.

At first, the marriage delighted me. The age difference of twenty-five years was far from a handicap as far as I was concerned. If anything, it was an inspiration. I was spending most of my time around young men so I didn't see why I couldn't be with a young woman, too.

Of course, there was a lot to put up with. Invariably, when we went out to dinner and there was any kind of music for dancing, some young fellow would come up and say, very respectfully, "Sir, may I have the honor of a dance with your daughter?" I was constantly being called away for phantom phone calls during which three or four fellows would try to hustle Barbara out of the place. I remember one ingenious guy I admired because he used a ploy that never would have occurred to me. He wrote his name and phone number on a napkin, folded it into a paper airplane and sailed it over to the table. There were also times when Barbara would enter an arena during a game and get a greater reception from the crowd than either team had received.

For a while, we travelled together, but when our daughter, Rena, was born, Barbara stayed at home in Munich. I began to learn the part missing from the old saying, "Absence makes the heart grow fonder." Which is, "as long as you don't come back."

I had been on the debating team in high school, but, between Barbara and her mother, I never came close to winning an argument. I don't know how often I heard how well, how intelligently and how efficiently things were done in Germany compared to the rest of the world. I was constantly hearing how the telephones worked better, the plumbing worked better, the cars worked better. It was terribly boring, especially since there was no reply because it was pretty much true.

There was no denying that Barbara was one of the most intelligent women I had ever met. One day I returned from the road to be told, "Put all your money into marks." It wasn't a request or a suggestion, but a direct order from the commander in chief. I resisted for a few days, but soon sleeping on the couch became uncomfortable so I converted all my cash. Three months later, the dollar was devalued and my money had doubled.

Another time, I booked some games in Manila when I had TWA as a sponsor. "Dumbkopf!" she screamed. "TWA doesn't fly to Manila. What you should do is play some games in Hong Kong and fly TWA. Then find another sponsor for the Philippines and bill them for the fare from America." That was an order that made me about $15,000.

I used to think that Hitler had made a mistake by not sending women to the Russian front instead of men. He might have won the war if he had.

The marriage lasted four years, which, as a matter of fact, was the length of my first one. Maybe that's all you can ask in the coaching business. The wives start with freshman eligibility, play through their senior years and then graduate. But as much as I regret what happened to Diane and me, I have no really strong feelings about my marriage to Barbara. I suppose when you marry a woman twenty-five years younger than you are, you can't expect to play Hamlet.

Besides, she gave me Rena and I will always be grateful for that.

After Barbara and I were divorced, I needed a full-time governess for Rena while I coached a club team in Gorizia, Italy. I was lucky to find Pina, a spinster who had dedicated her life to raising other people's children. But when we went on tour during the summer, Pina was reluctant to travel and I had to find a substitute. I chose one of my favorites, Monica, a six-foot blonde who had played on my national Swedish girl's team. Of course, I told her, I could not afford separate rooms for the three of us. She just smiled.

For a while, my biggest problem was keeping my players' minds on the game when Monica was around, but then real trouble came. The wife of one of the players decided she did not care for my arrangement at all. She was a Chinese woman who was always up to some sort of intrigue and everybody on the tour called her the Dragon Lady. She told Monica that her behavior was scandalous and before long a few of the other wives got into the act. Monica, who spent much of her time with the wives, eventually got quite upset.

But the final blow came when my assistant coach, who was from a New England college, made a strong pitch for her. He found out she wanted nothing in the world more than to go to college in the United States. I think he may be the only person I ever heard of who got a girl into bed by offering her a college scholarship. And I may be the only one who ever fired an assistant coach and a babysitter at the same time. I got pretty good at changing diapers by the time the tour was over and when fall came I was relieved to return to Gorizia and Pina.

CHAPTER 25

Africa Is Big and Dark, but at Least You Can Find a Place to Park

In 1968, the State Department asked me to coach the national team of Morocco. The basketball federation of that country wanted somebody who spoke French and that seemed to narrow it down to me. So, for the next few years, I was in and out of Africa on a regular basis. I probably logged more miles than Kissinger and with better results.

The Moroccan team was pretty fair and its top player, a big fellow named Said, was outstanding. Since his job was royal guard to King Hassan II, he was never late for practice, either. Later, he went on to play for several years with a Belgian club team. We practiced at night, which gave me a lot of free time during the day, and I was invited to use the royal golf course in Rabat. To say I had the course to myself was putting it mildly. There was the king and there was me. Never together.

I was somewhat surprised to discover that the president of the Moroccan federation was Jewish. We got along well and he invited me to his home several times. "I want you to meet my wife," he said the first time I was there. "I must apologize for being the only man of substance in Morocco who has only one."

The country was hosting the 1968 African basketball championships and the annual meeting of the African Basketball Federation was also being held there, in Casablanca. I was asked to attend all the official sessions to act as translator for the French- and English-speaking representatives. We assembled in a very grand hall and took up the first item on the agenda, which was to determine the site of the next African championships. A representative of one of the southern African nations asked to be recognized.

"After consulting with my fellow delegates from the black African countries," he said, "I would like to make a motion that, inasmuch as all the previous African championships have been held in Arab countries and while we appreciate the fact that the Arabs have done this, we feel it only right that the next championship be held in a black African country."

Nobody could argue with this logic; the motion passed unanimously without debate. Then the chairman asked which black African country would like to hold the tournament. There was total silence. None of the nations in question wanted the games, which can be an expensive proposition since national pride requires the building of a new arena. Apparently, none of the black African nations felt able to make the effort. It was an embarrassing situation, but I couldn't restrain myself.

"Unless the Arab countries are prepared to bid," I said, "shall we telephone South Africa?"

This drew a lot of laughter—even from the black African delegates—but no second. The previous motion had to be rescinded before they could pick a site and get on to other business.

The meeting soon bogged down because of the delegate from Guinea, who quickly became the most unpopular man there. Guinea was the only overtly communist country in Africa at the time and the delegate insisted on adding some political rider to every motion and working the party line into every issue, no matter how innocuous. He was far more concerned with colonialism and imperialism than he was with basketball. Even the delegates who agreed with his politics wanted only to get on with their business and play their tournament. After a day of listening to him, they decided to act.

The delegate from Guinea was attending the meeting without

a team. This was not uncommon because not all the countries felt their teams were strong enough to make a good showing, but most of them wanted to be in on federation business. During one session, while the delegate from Guinea was making another political statement, he was paged to take a telephone call.

A few moments later, he rushed back into the conference room and said, "Gentlemen, I beg to be excused. I have just received a call from the immigration officials at the airport. The national basketball team of my country has just arrived and their papers are not in order. I must go there to certify them and guide them through customs. This is a great surprise to me."

"Just a minute," the chairman of the meeting said, "we have already made up the complete calendar of games. The opening ceremonies are today at five P.M. and the first-round games are tomorrow. We now will have an uneven number of teams and we'll have to revise the schedule completely. I suppose your team will want one day of rest after its long journey, so this will be a tremendous job. I think you should revise the schedule—work it out with nine teams instead of eight—and please have it ready by eight o'clock tonight."

The president of the Moroccan federation then said, "Mr. McGregor, would you be so kind as to drive the distinguished delegate from Guinea to the airport to meet his team?"

All the way there, the delegate was so nervous that he could hardly sit still. As the car bumped along the dusty road, he tried to rearrange the schedule. This is hard enough if you've been around basketball for a while and almost impossible if you're as inexperienced as he was. When we got to the airport at Casablanca, it was nearly deserted. He became almost frantic when an airport official told him his team wasn't there and then reminded him there were two international airports in Morocco—the other two hours away at Rabat. I thought he was going to cry. But he came to me, wringing his hands at the thought of having to ask another favor of a representative of an imperialist colonialist state, and said, "Mr. McGregor, would you be kind enough to drive me to Rabat?"

I was just as puzzled as he was, but off we went to Rabat. When we got there, the airport was dark. There wasn't a soul around. I had a practice scheduled, so we raced back to Casablanca and I dropped him off, by then a complete nervous wreck. The next day at the convention, the president of the Moroccan federation came up to me, wearing a huge grin.

"Mac," he said, putting an arm around me, "I hope you didn't mind. But we had to get rid of that son of a bitch. And we couldn't send anybody else with him because we had to have enough votes to conduct business."

He told me the meeting had collapsed in laughter when the two of us had left, and then they had gone about their business. When that day's session was held, the delegate from Guinea was nowhere to be seen. Either he was too humiliated to show his face again or he was still looking for his team.

As for the tournament, Morocco did a fine job building an offense around Said and finished second, qualifying for the Olympics for the first and only time in its history. My six-month State Department assignment was up and, when the Moroccans asked that it be renewed long enough for me to take the team to Mexico City, they were told there had been a cut in the budget for such long-term exchange programs because of the expense of the Vietnam war. By then, I was almost resigned to missing the Olympics for one reason or another.

In 1968 and 1969, I did give short clinics in Gabon, Senegal and Nigeria and my instruction in Africa's basketball politics continued. In Gabon, I ran into trouble because France was jealous when any other countries tried to establish relationships with the newly independent African nations that had been French colonies. France still retained a number of advisers in many of those countries and continued to wield a great deal of influence. This became something of a problem when I was scheduled to give a clinic at a high school in Gabon. We arrived at the gym, only to find that it was dark and a key was needed to turn on the lights.

The principal of the school had a French adviser who encouraged him not to cooperate with this U.S. State Department clinic, so the people from the American Embassy had to go to the Ministry of Education. Soon, the question of whether or not to turn on the lights in a high school gym was referred to the highest chambers of government in the country. After sitting around for hours, we finally got the lights turned on, and the clinic took place.

In Senegal, I received a very warm welcome, though I was disappointed not to find the same reception committee that had greeted one of my touring teams a few years before. The Senegalese national dance troupe, a group of beautiful girls, had turned out at the Dakar airport. That they had been topless had not diminished their attraction one bit. For a while, I had been concerned that the game would never be played unless it was shifted to the airport. In fact, for those few days in Senegal, every time a plane landed, several of the players had rushed out to the airport to be on hand to greet the visitors.

I arrived in Nigeria to give some clinics just as the dispute between that country and Biafra was reaching the breaking point. Several weeks later, when I was down the coast in Gabon, civil war was declared. The French in Gabon were supporting the Biafran rebels, flying in war matériel and flying out those heart-rendingly malnourished children of whom we saw so many pictures.

I was staying in the same hotel as some of the pilots making these runs—they were mercenaries from other countries—and heard harrowing stories of attempts to land at makeshift Biafran airports that were little more than jungle clearings and were lit up for only a few minutes. If Nigerian troops were attacking, the lights could go out in the middle of a landing or sometimes the soldiers would try to decoy them by setting up lights where there were no landing strips.

When the children were brought to Gabon, there was no place to house them except refugee colonies on the beach where they were cared for by Biafran teachers and nurses—lovely young girls, most of them—who tried to continue the use of their own language and traditions even under such difficult circumstances.

As far as the eye could see down the beautiful Gabon beach, there were thousands and thousands of children, most of whom would never see their families again.

In 1970, I returned to Africa for my longest stay when the State Department asked me to coach the national team of the Central African Republic. This was an era when countries of every ideology were bidding for influence in Africa and it seemed that every sport imaginable was being taught by the representatives of one nation or another. There were coaches there from the Soviet Union, Czechoslovakia, Yugoslavia, Poland and Hungary, as well as a few holdovers from France.

Bangui, the capital of the Central African Republic, may well have been the most isolated one in the world. There were no railroads and the only decent highway leading to the city was a narrow two-lane road. The only really efficient way to reach the country from the outside was by air. Yet, the city was actually quite diverse by African standards, in part because of its horrifying history.

Central Africa was populated in large measure by tribes fleeing slave traders who worked along the African coast. No sooner did they escape traders capturing slaves for the Americas and West Indies than they ran into Arab slave merchants further inland. For hundreds of years, the leading export of this and surrounding areas was people.

In a museum at Bangui today, there is an item that resembles an oil drum, but which is actually a special invention of the Arabs. They would seal a man or a woman inside and then fling it into the river. The barrel would float downstream some 2,000 miles, and the survivor would find himself in slavery. Many died, but the Arabs figured that the time and expense saved in transporting their captives overland was worth the lost revenue. In later years, of course, rubber was discovered in the region and the Africans were forced to work on the plantations by the Belgians. There was always somebody ready and willing to enslave and murder them.

The revelation of my stay in the Central African Republic was the players. They had far more talent than I had expected, considering their brief exposure to the game. They had great speed, shot quite well and had a complete disregard for scrapes and bruises. They played the way we used to as kids, with everybody rushing in the direction of the ball at all times.

There were a couple of problems, though. Whoever had introduced the Central Africans to basketball—some Peace Corpsmen, perhaps—had neglected to mention that it was legal to use the left hand. Whether it was dribbling, shooting or passing, the Africans used their right hands only. Then, too, there were some aspects of the game that simply didn't interest them—passing, for instance, and finesse. It was impossible to get them to stay in their positions on the court and they were completely unsophisticated on defense. Every time somebody faked, the player guarding him would go for it—and so would his teammates, the players on the bench and a large portion of the fans as well.

But the Africans were brilliant at recovering loose balls—a good thing, because we caused a lot of them—and just as good at converting them into baskets. The bad pass soon became our best play. Defensively, we developed something unique—the five-on-one. Whichever member of the opposing team had the ball would soon find himself surrounded by the entire team and, more often than not, this resulted in another loose ball and another basket for us.

By and large, the players came from the small upper class and had been educated in French schools, but, in many ways, they weren't far removed from their tribal backgrounds. A player studying physics or advanced mathematics might be wearing some animal's tooth around his neck. When I'd ask about it, he'd say the witch doctor claimed it would protect him from bullets.

It wasn't always possible to make sure that a player was strictly eligible for the national team. Boundaries between African countries weren't always very well marked or patrolled so it wasn't unusual for a player on one team one year to show up representing another country the next. One of our best players, whose name was Bissini, had an extremely varied career. He was six feet ten and weighed 240, yet moved well enough to have been a star in any American league. His favorite shot was the dunk, which he would execute by taking off on the fly from the foul line, slamming the ball through the hoop, landing on his belly and sliding into the basket supports with a huge smile on his face. Then he would pick himself up and charge down the court for the next loose ball.

Bissini played for the Central African Republic one year, but then the Cameroons claimed him. The last I heard, he was playing in France, which allowed the residents of any of its former colonial possessions to claim French citizenship. He is another player who has served under three flags.

I had been coaching the Central African team for about a week when one of the players came up after practice and said they all wanted the following day off to go out into the jungle and hunt. He invited me to go along. All I knew about safaris was what I'd seen in Tarzan movies, so I scrounged around the hotel for the equipment I thought I'd need. The next morning, I showed up in my pith helmet, khaki shirt and pants and high boots, carrying an elephant gun and a carbine, with a couple of 45-caliber pistols strapped to my waist. When the jeep with the players pulled up, they took one look at me and broke out into hysterical laughter. They were all wearing shorts or jeans and most of them were barefoot. There wasn't a weapon in sight.

"What are you worried about?" one of them said when the laughter had died down.

"What am I worried about? There are elephants out there and hippopotamuses and lions and tigers and cheetahs and snakes."

"Don't worry," he said. "They won't bother you . . . if they've already eaten."

That made me feel much better, of course, and off we went into the jungle. They were still laughing hilariously when we ran into our first obstacle—a boa constrictor lying across the road sunning itself. The damn thing looked at least 100 feet long to me—though I suppose it was only 20 feet or so—and a yard thick. It had a huge bump in its coils; it must have just made a nice meal out of an animal. The driver pointed the jeep straight at the snake. Clearly, he meant to drive right over it.

"Wait a minute!" I screamed. "That thing could flip us right over!"

The players laughed again, but, to humor me, they stopped the jeep. I threw rocks at the snake to try to get him off the road, but this had no more effect than so many fleas. Finally, after much laughter and teasing at my expense, the boa slithered off into the ditch at the side of the road and we went on. It was then that I got my biggest shock of the day.

These young kids, armed only with clubs they picked up in the jungle, began to hunt. Their technique was simple: They simply ran the animals to death. Here they were, running through a territory filled with snakes and lizards and bugs and a thousand other wild creatures, chasing antelopes and wild deer until their prey tired. Then, with a blow over the head, the kill was made. All the time, I sat armed to the teeth in the safety of the jeep. Nothing in the world could have gotten me out of it. Thus did the great white hunter spend his safari in the African jungle.

However, I had no trouble living the life of a millionaire sportsman back in Bangui. I stayed in a small hotel that flanked a French sporting club with all the creature comforts a man could wish for—except one. As far as the number of available women were concerned, my entire time in Africa would have to be called "McGregor's Complaint."

There was a swimming pool and I put it to good use every morning, along with another man about my age who turned out to be the Russian ambassador. Whether consciously or unconsciously, we soon became involved in an unofficial competition. Early on, he would win because he had been there longer and had been swimming more regularly. Gradually, I began sneaking in evening workouts and catching up to him. Soon, he was joining me in the evening in order to maintain his edge.

This went on for about a month; the only acknowledgement we gave each other was a curt nod. One day, he spoke a word of greeting to me in Russian, which I returned in English. I was quite sure that he spoke not only English, but French as well, but eventually we compromised and exchanged a few words in German. Swimming can be a lonely and solitary sport and it was difficult for both of us not to enter into the spirit of détente.

During this period, some of the Soviet efforts in the Central African Republic were backfiring and relations between the two countries were less than cordial. A few African students had returned from Russia with some unkind words about their treatment there and this was followed by a break in the sports programs of the two countries. The day the Soviet volleyball coach was sent home, I suggested to the ambassador that he had better enjoy his tropical swimming while he could, because it might be considerably cooler at his next assignment. He was not amused. It was at least ten nautical miles before we exchanged greetings again.

One of the crowning achievements of my athletic career occurred while I was in Bangui. I became the golf champion of the Central African Republic. I won the title fair and square against the entire golfing population of the country, which, at the time, numbered seven.

The lone golf course in the country had been hacked right out of the jungle, and a player was accompanied around it by both a caddy and beaters, whose duty it was to scare away snakes in the rough. Actually, the fairways themselves resembled the roughs of most golf courses. When you hit the ball off the course, you had the choice of leaving it there, which meant a two-stroke penalty, or trying to find it in the jungle, in which case the stakes could be considerably higher. The greens consisted of sand and had to be rolled rather than trimmed.

The contestants in the national tournament included the defending champion—who had designed the course and kept a cheetah chained up in his front yard adjoining it—several ambassadors, who were almost as old as their clubs, and me. I felt like a combination of Jack Nicklaus and Colonel Blimp as I scored an eighty-five, losing only two balls and one beater along the way and finishing with the winning card. I have often wondered if I could have applied to compete in the Master's on the strength of this victory.

Bangui drew a lot of visitors from all over Africa while I was there; the city seemed to be a stopping-off point for Arab traders and African peasants on their way elsewhere. The American cowboys, who became a legend in the Old West for moving cattle along the Chisholm Trail, were nothing compared to the cowboys from Chad who drove their animals all through Africa, thousands of miles across the desert. By the time they arrived in the Central African Republic, the cattle were little more than skeletons. The drovers would stay for a while, fatten up their herds on the water and feed that was plentiful in Bangui and then be off again.

The Europeans used a Bangui as a starting point for their safaris. They would fly in on their private jets, immaculately attired in the latest hunting fashions purchased in Paris, and stay at one of the few decent hotels before going into the jungle. There were certain times of the year when, with the Arabs, the Africans and the Europeans, you would see every type of dress imaginable on the streets of Bangui.

I had just begun to get used to these sights when one summer day a small caravan of jeeps pulled into the city. The men in them were white and their khaki clothes were as caked with grime and sand as their vehicles. I thought they must be part of some movie company on location until I heard them speaking German.

"Where did you come from?" I asked one of them.

"Across the Sahara," he said.

"*Across the Sahara? By jeep?* But there aren't any roads! There are huge windstorms! And the heat must be unbelievable in the summer! You guys are crazy!"

He just laughed. "We were in the Afrika Corps during the war," he said. "We're on holiday."

I couldn't believe it, but it was true enough. Every summer, former German soldiers would organize a jeep trip that took about twenty days across the Sahara to relive their days in World War II. They used compasses to navigate, stayed in and around Bangui until their vacations were over and then loaded the jeeps on a plane, flying them back to northern Africa before returning to Germany. Every ten or twelve days during the summer, another contingent of three or four jeeps would roll into town, covered with sand and filled with former members of the Afrika Corps.

Even so, the Central African Republic may have been the only country in the world that didn't make any real money from German tourists. They didn't even stay in any of the hotels; they preferred to camp out and sit around the fire singing German songs, reliving their wartime experiences.

While I coached in the Central African Republic, the team competed in one African championship tournament, at Dakar, and finished a creditable third. But by far our most triumphant moments on the court came, not in Africa, but on a tour of Europe that was one of the most delightful trips I have ever taken. I have generally had good luck taking foreign teams to Europe; the fans there are naturally curious about players from other parts of the world and therefore we usually draw well. But the impression made by the Central African team during its tour of Sweden, Germany and the Netherlands in 1971, exceeded all my expectations. The team played about forty games and was a sensation.

The European fans went wild when they saw the enthusiastic, uninhibited play of the Africans. Their complete abandon delighted the audiences and befuddled the European players. Some poor German player would get the ball and suddenly find himself surrounded by five hyperactive kids waving their hands in his face. He had never before encountered anything like it and, when he would try to pass, somebody would knock the ball away, pick it up and race in for a basket. We won thirty-two or thirty-three of the games, remarkable for a team that had never even witnessed the game played outside of Africa. We beat the national team of the Netherlands and lost to the German national team by just one point.

The players were fascinated by Europe, particularly by the fact that there were no flies. I didn't have the heart to tell them this was only because it was winter. They enjoyed the European food as well, but that didn't stop them from bringing along a little something from home. Everywhere we went, they dragged along huge sacks containing something that resembled mashed sweet potatoes. And no matter where they had eaten dinner—be it the most elegant of European restaurants—they would return to their rooms at night for a snack.

Toward the end, as the supply of food grew low and the cold weather began to weigh on them, the players began to get a little homesick and irritable. But all in all, I believe I never enjoyed a tour of Europe more.

We returned home to a huge welcome. The Central African authorities were delighted with the attention we had received in Europe. I was given the *Mérite Sportive* by the government, and the players received cash bonuses that would have upset the international basketball federation if it had known. Soon, there was a clamor for us to play some exhibition games. Since basketball was on everybody's mind, the sports council decided to break with precedent by holding the game at night and selling tickets. In the past, whatever games the national team played had been free and in the daytime.

Now, there are aspects of equatorial Africa that must be understood. The sun comes up at the same time every day and goes down at the same time every night. Today is like yesterday and tomorrow will be like today. There are some places where it even rains at almost exactly the same time every day. And, since you don't have to work all summer to get ready for a barren winter, there isn't always a lot of long-range planning.

So I wasn't too surprised that when officials put up a ticket booth at the basketball court the night of our exhibition and placed a guy inside with a roll of tickets, they forgot one little thing—a fence. The whole town just converged on the place from every direction and sat down in the bleachers. I don't think a single ticket was sold. Not that it really mattered. They would have had to refund all the money, anyhow.

There was a nice little ceremony, beginning at dusk, welcoming the team back from Europe. Then the lights that had been set up for the game were turned on. If you turn on floodlights in Portland, Oregon, on a warm evening, you'll attract some moths and bugs, but you'll still be able to play tennis or basketball or whatever. But if you suddenly light up the jungle, you'll attract, by conservative estimate, a billion bugs. And you won't be able to play anything because you'll be spending every moment protecting yourself from bugs.

I opened my mouth to say something and found there were bugs in it, as well as in my eyes, ears and nose. There was no way the game could be played. The lights were turned off and everybody went home. I believe that still stands as the only game ever to be called because of bugs.

The game was rescheduled for a week or so later in the daytime. In the intervening period, there was a tremendous rainfall which weakened the earth under one part of the floor and resulted in a little valley right out there on the court. This made for some interesting strategy. A player would go out on a fast break, drop down out of sight in the valley and then pop up behind the defense to catch a long pass and score.

All this has changed now. They have built an excellent arena at Bangui and have hosted two or three major international events. None of them has been disturbed by bugs as far as I know.

CHAPTER **26**

Keep It Simple

I SOMETIMES WONDER which will go first—the tour or me. The first time you spend 100 different nights in 100 different beds, it's exciting. The second time, it's routine. The third time, you notice the lumps in the mattress. And after a while, the missionary zeal disappears as well. With McDonald's on the Champs-Élysées and Coca-Cola a staple in the heart of Africa, I have become less enthralled than I once was with my role as an exporter of American culture. Now that I have been to the four corners of the earth, my curiosity is less than it once was, too.

When I can take Rena, who is ten now, with me, some of the old joy of travel for its own sake returns. I find vicarious pleasure in watching her discover new places and cultures for the first time. But otherwise, the lure of the other side of the mountain has lessened over the years; the problems of the tour, once such a challenge, have become less exciting as I face them over and over again.

In the spring of 1977, I found myself in the warmth of France, thinking about that old Christmas movie, *Miracle on 34th Street*. But what I needed was a miracle on Nice's Promenade des Anglais. We were about to begin a twenty-game tour of Italy with only five players. The news from the home front was that, of the other players who were supposed to join us, one was still trying to decide, another had changed his mind on the way to the airport, a third was going to be three days late and a fourth had been intercepted by a competitor.

This sort of thing can be extremely nerve-racking, even though it always seems to work out somehow. Once, we wound up a tour at the Christmas tournament in Amsterdam, a traditional event that is televised and receives a great deal of publicity. Several of my players wanted to get home for the holidays, but I wasn't concerned. Many of the players in Europe gather in Amsterdam around that time and are available to play in the tournaments.

This time, I had miscalculated. With no more than half an hour to go before we were to take the court for a televised game, I was sitting in the locker room with only four players. I was about to suffer perhaps the most embarrassing public moment of my career, one that would damage my reputation severely.

Suddenly, the door to the locker room flew open and Ken Grant strolled in.

"Hi, Coach," he said. "Just got in from Sweden. Got a uniform for me?"

"Well, you're late, Kenny," I said, trying to stifle a grin. "But I think we can squeeze you in."

Within moments, the door opened four more times and in walked Tom Chestnut, Fran O'Hanlon, Tom Austin and Billy Banks. They were among the best players I had ever had and were all in top shape from a season of basketball at their various clubs. We won the tournament in a breeze. I had been saved to fight the battle another day.

I also worry increasingly that the tour, like the great ocean liners, may be becoming obsolete. Television in Europe, which played such a big role in our public acceptance, may kill us off in the long run. It's a tough competitor on a rainy night when a telecast of two top club teams competes with our game against a local club. With costs rising, we have to schedule five or six games a week just to break even and television makes this more and more difficult.

Lately, I can see that my attitude toward my team has changed, too. It was once so intense that I would run to the water fountain faster than my players got down the court. I had learned the truth of what an older coach at Benson High in Portland, where I got my first job, had told me when he saw me using a lot of complicated techniques.

"Mac, for God's sake," he would say. "Keep it simple. You don't have the smartest guys in town here. Stop trying to run all these plays. Just teach the skills. You've got a tremendously contagious enthusiasm and the kids will believe in you and go out and hustle if you don't complicate it too much."

I thought he was Mr. Yesterday, thirty years behind the times, but gradually I came around to see that "keep it simple" was the best advice. Basic skills, the willingness to work and desire could carry a team a long way. Those were the elements I tried to impart. My effectiveness as a coach seemed to be in direct proportion to the amount of nervous energy and intensity I could summon up and transmit to my players. The teams I was proudest of were invariably the ones that I had gotten to play the hardest and with the greatest determination.

But, lately, I've begun to relax, to compromise a bit. I guess I've come to the conclusion that my own health and sanity are more important than squeezing every last victory out of the schedule. I'm lucky because I don't have any championships to win; my season doesn't rise or fall with each victory as it does for the coaches in American colleges or in the NBA. Coaching on that level is the most pressure-packed occupation I know. Very often, the men who enter it get out at relatively young ages when they realize it's either another line of work for them or a heart attack.

Just a few years after winning an NBA championship in Los Angeles, Bill Sharman left coaching without regret. The pressures of maintaining the intensity needed to compete effectively on the professional level, coupled with the deaths of his wife and his father, were the reasons. These pressures also reached Alex Hannum, one of the top coaches in professional basketball for a number of years. Pete Newell also quit at a relatively young age, and recently it was Al McGuire. I'm interested to see how long Bobby Knight, the volcanic young coach at the University of Indiana, can keep it up.

If I had a son who was interested in coaching basketball, I would do the best I could to talk him out of it. The odds against survival, against reaching retirement age, are simply too great. For every John Wooden, who goes out with a testimonial banquet, there are hundreds of coaches who walk or are driven away. I know, of course, that young men wanting to go into coaching will no more heed this advice than I would have, had it been given to me thirty years ago. Therefore, I have formulated McGregor's Ten Commandments for anyone contemplating a career as a basketball coach:

1. Marry rich. Career decisions based on money alone can lead to a lifetime of regret.

2. Get fired as soon and as often as possible. This will provide you with invaluable experience in applying for new positions.

3. Remember the Golden Rule. Friends are more important than victories. Besides, the people you leave behind may still be there when you come back.

4. Adjust your tactics to meet the situation. On tour, our policy was always to steal the ball, then shoot it before the home-town referees knew we had it and could take it away. And, from a showmanship point of view, we would never stall. We would rather lose the game than the crowd.

5. Don't be too nice a guy. Athletic directors and general managers want qualified coaches, but also somebody they can fire. If they think people are going to be overly sorry for you when you are fired, you may not get the job in the first place.

6. Prepare an alternative career and be prepared to practice it.

7. Cultivate the sportswriters. A current phenomenon makes this easier than it used to be. The coach can now marry the sportswriter.

8. Develop a high tolerance for boredom. Successful coaching

consists of endless repetition of boring fundamentals. Some players grasp the idea "catch the ball with both hands" the first time they hear it. Others don't on the hundredth. Also, falling asleep at practice is bad form.

9. Be versatile. This is especially important in high school and college. As a case in point, I offer my one and only experience as a baseball coach which occurred during my stay at Whitworth.

The regular baseball coach was sick on the day his team was scheduled to play a traditional rival. I was asked to be his replacement, despite the fact that my ignorance of the game was exceeded only by my lack of interest in it. Nevertheless, we made it as far as the ninth inning with the score tied. With the bases loaded and one out, our poorest hitter and slowest runner was at the plate, so I told him to go up without a bat. I figured he might get hit by a pitch or he might walk or he might be called out on strikes. But at least he wouldn't be able to hit into a double play, which would end the game.

The opposing pitcher was so flustered at the sight of a hitter without a bat that he threw three straight balls. Then his coach protested that a batter had to have a bat. I didn't have a rulebook, but the umpires did and they could find no such rule. The other coach topped this by saying, "This is my field and I say you have to have a bat."

The umpires responded to such unassailable logic by ordering me to give the hitter a bat. I refused. The argument continued until it was dark and the game was called a tie. Upon hearing what had transpired, the regular Whitworth baseball coach immediately recovered from his illness and I returned to coaching basketball.

10. Keep it simple.

If I'm ever able to give up or cut down on the travelling, my summer basketball camp at Long Beach may be a big reason. I've been fairly successful in attracting foreign players, and some countries have sent me their entire national teams. It gives them the opportunity to see how basketball is played in this country, to get instruction from visiting coaches like Bobby Knight and Pete Newell and to avail themselves of such traditional American cultural attractions as Disneyland and Hollywood.

Though the profit margin in running an operation like this is high—$200 for everyone who stays for three weeks—the camp season is short, so the total returns are limited. Either I will have to enlarge the operation in future years or find something else that will keep me at home.

Very recently, I thought I might have hit on it when I came close to marrying for a third time. While I was at my mother's house in Portland early in 1977, I met a charming, intelligent widow. She had a lovely home by the golf course, enough money for two to live on comfortably and a twelve-year-old son who was just right for Rena. I had warm visions of a nice, quiet life with my family around me, golf on each day with less than three feet of rain and no trip further than to the supermarket.

Alas, the lady's ideas were different. After a life as a wife and mother, distant horizons were calling, and I seemed as convenient a vehicle for the realization of her dreams as she did for mine. Her son would be sent to boarding school, Rena would stay with my mother and the lady would tour with me and the team. As ready as I was for a life in the suburbs, she wanted one of adventure. The romance ended quickly when she took off on a world cruise, while I sat home and looked wistfully through home and garden magazines. In a few months, she was back in Portland and I was on the road again.

Well, the book is over, but the story is not. I would kind of like to know how it's going to end myself. In the meantime, I've just heard of a tournament that will be held soon in Outer Mongolia. I'm hoping to schedule Bhutan, Nepal and Tibet en route.

Index